Rottweilers

Dr. Herbert Richards

Edited by the Staff of T.F.H. Publications

Front cover photo by Robert Pearcy.

Back cover: *Upper left:* Canadian Ch. Kyladie's Avitar the Wiz, CD, at nine months of age. Owned by Mr. Aime and Mrs. Adele Brosseau. *Upper right:* The eight-week-old puppy Thor von Germelshausen, bred and owned by Mrs. Betty Bilsky. *Bottom left:* Puppies from the Noblehaus Kennels of Mark and Patricia Schwartz and Gabor Brichter. *Bottom Right:* Nello von Stolzenfels, bred by the Ellmans and owned by John Wahl, shown at the age of seven months.

The Chapter "The History of the Rottweiler" has been reprinted from *The Book of the Rottweiler,* by Anna Katherine Nicholas, copyright 1981 by T.F.H. Publications, Inc.

Distributed in the UNITED STATES by T.F.H. Publications, Inc., 211 West Sylvania Avenue, Neptune City, NJ 07753; in CANADA by H & L Pet Supplies Inc., 27 Kingston Crescent, Kitchener, Ontario N2B 2T6; Rolf C. Hagen Ltd., 3225 Sartelon Street, Montreal 382 Quebec; in ENGLAND by T.F.H. Publications Limited, 4 Kier Park, Ascot, Berkshire SL5 7DS; in AUSTRALIA AND THE SOUTH PACIFIC by T.F.H. (Australia) Pty. Ltd., Box 149, Brookvale 2100 N.S.W., Australia; in NEW ZEALAND by Ross Haines & Son, Ltd., 18 Monmouth Street, Grey Lynn, Auckland 2 New Zealand; in SINGAPORE AND MALAYSIA by MPH Distributors (S) Pte., Ltd., 601 Sims Drive, # 03/07/21, Singapore 1438; in the PHILIPPINES by Bio-Research, 5 Lippay Street, San Lorenzo Village, Makati Rizal; in SOUTH AFRICA by Multipet Pty. Ltd., 30 Turners Avenue, Durban 4001. Published by T.F.H. Publications Inc., Ltd. the British Crown Colony of Hong Kong.

Contents

Poster A: A typical Rottweiler portrait by Robert Pearcy.
Poster B: Ch. Bratiana's Manfried B'Yisroel RO 2812 shown by his owner-handler Trish Ransom of Fremont, California.
Poster C: A typical Rottweiler portrait by Robert Pearcy.

Introduction

The proper introduction to a book like this one is a list of other good books about dogs, because no relatively small book could hope to cover comprehensively all of the specialized topics that a serious dog fancier can become involved with. Breeding, training, exhibiting, health care—they're all important topics, each one deserving a big volume of its own for proper exposition. The following books are all published by T.F.H. Publications and are recommended to you for additional information.

Dog Behavior, Why Dogs Do What They Do by Dr. Ian Dunbar (H-1016) is a thorough and enlightening exploration of all aspects of canine behavior and the relationship between man and dog. The author, a noted specialist in the field of animal behavior, discusses canine communication, social and sexual behaviors, and the physical and sensory capacities and capabilities of dogs, among other topics.

How to Train Your Dog by Ernest H. Hart (PS-644) is a basic training manual which teaches the quickest and easiest route to canine training.

Dog Training by Lew Burke (H-962) reveals the secrets behind the methods successfully used by the author, a premier trainer of dogs for individuals, industry, and the government. Lew Burke concentrates on understanding dogs' needs in relation to the needs of their owner, and he uses dogs' psychological makeup to keep dogs happy by being obedient.

All About Dog Shows by Sam Kohl (PS-778) is a highly informative as well as entertaining introduction to dog shows. Written for the visitor to a dog show and for the beginning exhibitor, the book is illustrated with satirical pen-and-ink sketches of dogs and their exhibitor-owners.

Successful Dog Show Exhibiting by Anna Katherine Nicholas (H-993) is an excellent how-to manual for purebred dog owners who are thinking about entering the world of dog show competition. The book includes detailed explanations of dog show classes, step-by-step descriptions of the judging process (including what the judge looks for), ring behavior do's and don'ts for both dog and handler, and advantages and disadvantages of professional handlers versus showing your own dog. The author, a judge who's been part of the world of dogs for over 50 years, knows her subject well and makes it understandable for the reader.

Dog Breeding by Ernest H. Hart (H-958) is an easy-to-read account of

Introduction

all the things a person needs to know about mating dogs to upgrade the breed. The mechanics, techniques, and results of breeding, the physiology of the bitch and stud dog, gestation, whelping, fertility, how to build a strain, and how genetics can actually be used by the breeder are among the subjects covered in detail by the author.

Dog Breeding for Professionals by Dr. Herbert Richards (H-969) is a straightforward discussion of how to breed dogs of various sizes and how to care for newborn puppies. The many aspects of breeding (including possible problems and practical solutions) are covered in great detail. The explicit photos of canine sexual activities may offend some readers.

Dog Owner's Encyclopedia of Veterinary Medicine by Allan H. Hart, B.V.Sc. (H-934) is a comprehensive treatise on canine disease and disorders. It is written on the premise that dog owners should recognize the symptoms and understand the treatments of most diseases of dogs, so that dog owners can properly communicate with their veterinarian or give treatment to their dogs. Proper nutrition, parasite problems, and first-aid measures are also described.

• • •

In addition to the foregoing, the following individual breed books of interest to readers of this book are available at pet shops and book stores.

**THE BOOK OF THE ROTTWEILER
By Anna Katherine Nicholas**
ISBN 0-87666-735-3
TFH H-1035

This book is for those dedicated Rottweiler owners and breeders who never get enough of seeing or learning about their breed. Anna Katherine Nicholas, a well-known judge for 50 years, has been in touch with most of the leading breeders in the country in order to research and obtain photos for this book, including those names that have been familiar in the breed for decades. For those experienced Rottweiler fanciers, this book will provide a thorough update to their knowledge of the breed. For novices, it will open a vast new dimension of owning/breeding/ showing and provide an exhaustive reference book for sources and general information for years to come.
*Hard cover, 5½ x 8", 544 pages
Illustrated with 89 full-color photos;
378 black and white photos.*

History and Origins of the Dog

Where there are people there are dogs. Whether they are stray dogs roaming the alleys of an eastern town, sheepdogs in mountain pastures, or purebred toy dogs living luxuriously in a modern western city, dogs undoubtedly like to be near people.

People like dogs too. They like them for all sorts of reasons—because they do a good job for them, guarding their homes and property, herding their livestock, keeping down vermin, or hunting and retrieving game. People like a dog because he's fun to be with, a good companion to share a game, a walk, or a warm fire, and a friendly creature who thinks his human master is just great.

The bond between man and dog is a unique relationship. There is no other quite the same between man and other domesticated animals. Man keeps sheep and cattle, ducks and chickens because they are useful in providing food, but the deep friendship, the reliance on one another, is not there. The horse perhaps builds up some relationship with his human master, but with rare exceptions it isn't real friendship—mostly it is based on trainability through physical contact with man, and on the reward of sugar and oats. Horses are basically still wild animals at heart—they don't particularly want a human friend.

Cats come and go in the human home; sometimes they get very fond of their human friends, but however long the cat lives with people, it retains its independence. Its devotion is based mainly on an appreciation of the food and warmth that it gets from man. If they go, so does the cat. It too remains basically a wild animal, but one intelligent enough to appreciate that food and shelter can come the easy way. Nevertheless, if it has to, it is perfectly capable of leading an independent existence.

Children keep hamsters, rabbits, pigeons, rats and mice and even insects as pets—but the devotion is usually more on the human side than the animals'.

With dogs, it's different. The affection between man and dog is mutual. We love 'em as much as they love us.

Yet for all this close companionship, this mutual devotion which has existed for such an incredibly long time, we know very little about the history and origins of the dog. To give him a

History and Origins of the Dog

scientific label, the dog is a member of the genus *Canis*.

We know, from fossils mostly, that the dog's immediate ancestors probably existed about half a million years ago.

Early Origins

Nobody really knows for sure, but it is thought that the history of the dog began, in a remote sort of way, as long ago as 40 million years. There was a small family of carnivores (meat-eaters) then called *Miacidae*.

The *Miacidae* family had two descendants, one called *Daphaenus*, which eventually gave rise to the bears. The other was called *Cynodictis*, and was a smaller creature. From this creature there eventually evolved a dog-like animal called *Tomarctus*, which is thought to be the ancestor of dogs, wolves and jackals.

In the past it was often believed that the wolf and the jackal were the ancestors of the dog. All three are scientifically classified as being in the *Canis* family, but it has now been accepted by some authorities, that, though they are related, they are all separate offshoots of

Tomarctus. Other authorities hold that our dogs are descendants of the wolf.

Of course it is a long way from *Tomarctus*, the granddaddy of them all, to the modern dog that we know. *Tomarctus* had descendants. They developed differently in different places. Thousands of years went by, and sometime during this period man-like creatures met dog-like creatures.

All of this is unrecorded, and the sparse information available is based mostly on the evidence of geologists and archeologists working from fossilized remains.

They can given an approximate date for a type of prehistoric dog living domestically. It is placed between 6000 and 3000 B.C. A portion of the remains of a dog of no specific breed were found buried next to the remains of a woman on the coast of Zeeland.

There have also been archeological discoveries of domesticated dogs in Switzerland and in several other places, all prehistoric.

From this authorities conclude that dogs must have been domesticated in other parts of the world during those periods. As evolution takes such a long time, it is reasonable to suppose dogs must

History and Origins of the Dog

have been living in some kind of association with man many thousands of years before that.

They say that domestication could have taken place any time from 50,000 to 250,000 years ago. This would make the dog a very old friend indeed.

Man and Dog Meet

How did man and dog become associated in the first place? Since we've agreed it must have happened long before the time of recorded history, we can only guess. Both primitive man and primitive dog were hunters. Their paths must have crossed sometime or another. Perhaps man on one of his hunting expeditions caught a dog and used it for food—and kept on hunting it.

Maybe primitive man came across a female dog with puppies at some time, took them home to his cave or hole and kept them because he found that they could be fattened up for better eating. Perhaps playing outside the cave one day, Junior primitive man's son and heir, and his baby sisters found that the puppies romped and played rather attractively, and primitive man and his wife watched indulgently.

Somehow, somewhere, perhaps in several places in the world around about the same time, primitive man discovered that the dog was more than just another wild animal to be hunted, killed and eaten.

He discovered that instead of being a rival on the hunt for food, the dog would go along and help. He discovered that the dog would make a noise, give warning when danger approached. He discovered that the young of dogs were attractive play companions for his own young, that if the puppies grew up in the human encampment they became friendly and affectionate.

The dog too probably discovered that food was easier to come by in the vicinity of humans. The odd bone that primitive man threw over his shoulder when he'd finished with it probably gave primitive dog hours of pleasure chewing. Perhaps a chance incident like that was the first step ever in animal training—the first time mankind discovered that there were ways other than killing to bring an animal under control.

Why the dog should be willing to stay near man instead of running away as all other animals would do is one of these freaks of nature. It is a freak that has paid good dividends to both.

History and Origins of the Dog

How Different Breeds Originated

We've already said that either *Tomarctus*, the dog-like animal, or the wolf was probably the ancestor of the true dog, which is known scientifically as *Canis familiaris*. *Canis familiaris* developed into various forms.

The earliest date that can be put to a specific type is about 4000 B.C., which is the date given to the remains of *Canis familiaris palustris* which were found around the Swiss Lakes. Any of the various types of *Canis familiaris* could be earlier or later. Nobody knows for certain. Perhaps in the future more archeological searches will turn up new evidence that will tell us more. Otherwise, the farthest back we can go is to the beginning of recorded history, which is 4000 to 3000 B.C. There is evidence that a greyhound type of dog like the Saluki, and a Mastiff type were in existence then. There are representations of them both on an ancient green slate tablet which was found at Thebes and dates back to 4000 B.C.

On some tombs of ancient Egypt, dating back to 2200 to 2000 B.C., there are depicted hunting hounds of the Saluki type, as well as a heavier, mastiff-like dog, and a hunting dog with prick ears and a tightly curled tail not unlike a bigger, longer bodied Basenji. These tombs also show some dogs shorter in the legs and with thicker coats.

There is a dark-coated one with a tassled tail, and another with a spotted pattern marking and a curled tail.

The Effects of Nature

All dogs started off as hunters, but they would hunt different kinds of prey, depending on where they lived. Where the natural animals of the area were fast moving creatures, then the dogs would have to develop the kind of body that would move even faster—like the lean sight-hunting breeds of the greyhound type who can spot a moving object a long way away and chase it at terrific speed.

Where the natural animals lived in dense cover, in forests, with plenty of undergrowth, then the hunting dog would need to have a good tracking nose to seek out his food. Where the prey lived in burrows underground, the dog after his dinner would need to have not only a good nose but the instinct to dig

9

History and Origins of the Dog

down into the ground. Dogs hunting big animals would need to be bigger and fiercer to combat their adversaries.

Climate too would make a difference. Dogs living in the cold parts of Northern Europe and North America would need thick, dense coats to survive the icy conditions. Dogs that lived in thick forests and jungles would need to be smooth coated because a long coat would tangle in the undergrowth. Dogs in hot climates would develp short coats for coolness.

Man and dog teamed up, as we have seen, and man found that the dog could be useful. Eventually he would discover that the different kinds of dog could do different jobs. So man started to dabble in the development of the dog. He kept some kinds of dogs for hunting, some for guarding his property.

As man grew more civilized and started to keep animals around his encampment to raise for food instead of having to go out and hunt for meat all the time, he discovered that dogs could be used to guard his livestock, and then to herd them for him.

Gradually, under man's guidance, physical qualities and qualities of temperament and character began to be developed and fixed.

The Appearance of Breeds

Most of the early dogs had a natural length of nose and width of head. Quite early in the history of dogs, however, another kind of dog appeared. This is the dwarf. This does not mean a miniature. The proportions of any miniature are exactly like the bigger version; only the size varies. A true dwarf, however, is quite different. The limbs and body are foreshortened and malformed, giving an abnormal appearance. How these dwarfs first appeared is not known. It was probably by what is called mutation. Mutations are one of the mysteries of nature—they just happen. Very little about how and why they happen naturally is known.

Enough of these dwarfs survived, and produced their own kind, to influence the varieties of dogs. How long it took we do not know, but there are signs of dwarfed ancestry in any breed which has crooked front legs, loosened folds of skin, squashed-up face, and very broad, domed skulls.

Man has of course encouraged some of these features, mostly perhaps because they appealed to him. Man has mixed them up and introduced them into other breeds. As a result you have such varying

History and Origins of the Dog

kinds of dog as the Bloodhound, the Boxer, the Bulldog, the Basset Hound, the Welsh Corgi, the Pug, the Pekingese, the Japanese Spaniel, and many more, all of which show some signs of having "dwarf" characteristics, perhaps introduced a long, long way back in their ancestry. Small dogs like the Pekingese are the most obvious examples of an almost complete dwarf dog, deliberately bred that way by man.

Dogs like the Chihuahua and the Miniature Pinscher and the Toy Poodle are not dwarfs. They are midgets—miniatures—exact replicas of their bigger relatives. Small specimens occur in any living thing, including people. In dogs, man has deliberately encouraged the miniature and "bred down" to it.

As man continued to develop his civilization, he continued to create new breeds of dogs to suit his various needs. Man also moved about the world more easily, and dogs moved with him so that dogs from different kinds of places were interbred. Some kinds of dogs became extinct; new kinds were created. Some kinds of dogs remained basically the same for thousands of years.

It is thought that there are at present between 400 and 500 distinct breeds of dog in the world. In another hundred years there might be more or less. Many of them are man-made. The dog has come a long way from old *Cynodictis*. He probably still has a long way to go. In all that changing, one thing has remained unchanged, and that is the strength of the dog's unique relationship with man.

The Dog at Work

We've seen that the earliest work the dog did, some thousands of years ago, was to work alongside primitive man, first in hunting, then as watchdog, guard of his master's property, home and livestock, and later in herding his livestock.

Very early in their history dogs were also a form of food and in some parts of the world they were raised, and still are raised, to provide meat.

Throughout the centuries, the dog's usefulness to man has extended, until today it reaches very sophisticated and advanced forms.

Hunting dogs can be classed among the oldest. In ancient Babylonia, and in the Egypt of the Pharaohs, they were highly valued for this. They include the "sight-hounds"—fast greyhound types; the

History and Origins of the Dog

"scent-hounds"—heavier and slower, and usually hunted in packs or groups. Getting nearer to modern times the short-legged terriers and small breeds like the Dachshund, which go to earth and drive the prey above ground for the scent-hounds to kill; and finally the sporting dogs, the pointers and setters, the retrievers and spaniels, all of whom assist man by finding and retrieving, while their master does the actual killing with his gun.

The guarding dogs are almost as old as the hunters. They defend their master and his property. Mostly they are big breeds, starting with the Molussus of olden times, developing into the Mastiff, the sheep-guarding kinds like the Komondor, and the heavy coated dogs of the Greek mountains.

Guard dogs generally, though, are not uncontrollable, vicious animals. To make the best use of them mankind had to temper their fierceness and power with intelligence. Powerful guard dogs have always had the reputation of never attacking on sight, but only when the intruder interferes with their master's property, their master's person, or attacks the dog himself. The culmination of man's efforts in breeding this kind of dog is seen in the modern guard dog, the wonderfully trainable German Shepherd Dog, and the supremely efficient Doberman Pinscher.

In early times, the massive guard breeds were used in actual battle. Big and fierce, they were made even more ferocious looking with spiked collars, and they were protected by special suits of armor. Dogs were used for fighting as late as the 16th and 17th centuries.

The modern war dog is a different type—his value lies not just in his size and fierceness but primarily in his intelligence. Dogs have been trained for sentry duty, for scout work, for messenger duty, for patrol work, and as sled and pack dogs. With their marvelous olfactory abilities they were particularly successful in things like mine detection!

Modern war dogs don't need to be as massive as their ancient Mastiff predecessors. Mostly they have been German Shepherds, Doberman Pinschers, Giant Schnauzers, Airedales, farm Collies, and even Dalmatians.

At home, the shepherding and droving dogs did, and still do, provide wonderful service to their masters. There are the Collies, of various kinds, the cattle dogs like the Australian Kelpies, and the little Welsh Corgi among others.

History and Origins of the Dog

Some heavy breeds of dogs can draw light carts, and they were used for this on the continent of Europe a lot at one time, although in recent years that use has declined. The dogs of the Arctic, the sled dogs like the Huskies and Samoyed, still work in harness in snowy wastelands.

Dogs as Useful Companions

Less obvious in its usefulness is the dog's value as a companion. The first people who kept dogs probably didn't rate this aspect very high, but certainly from the time history began to be recorded there is evidence that people found joy in the company of a dog.

Cheops, the great Egyptian pyramid builder, left sculptures of his favorite hound, as did other Egyptian Pharaohs. So it went on over the centuries, as many literary works and works of art reveal. In the books and pictures of the famous there often appears a beloved dog. Today newspapers frequently feature heart-rending stories about a boy and his dog, or a picture of the Queen of England or the President of the United States with canine companions.

Perhaps the most selfless and honorable work that the dog has ever done for the human race is the work of the Seeing Eye dogs and Guide Dogs for the Blind. These intelligent and sensitive dogs are virtually the eyes of their blind masters or mistresses. Using a specially designed harness, they will guide their human charges unerringly and safely through busy streets, heavy traffic and congested sidewalks. They give their owners confidence in strange places and buildings, and they are taught not only to respond to commands but also to substitute their own initiative and judgment if necessary to insure the blind person's safe conduct.

Of course a strong bond of affection grows between sighted dog and blind master or mistress, perhaps the closest ever in the associated history of dog and man. It is so strong and devoted that the only heart-breaking part about it all is when the dog gets too old to carry on.

Symbolisms of the Dog

The very qualities that make the dog such a good worker and companion to man, are the ones that have given rise to his use in religion. With his superior sense of smell and hearing, the dog warns his master of danger, and protects

History and Origins of the Dog

him and his property from harm. Thus the dog becomes a symbol of protection against all kinds of evil. Symbolism is an essential part of any religion. To Christians, for instance, the cross is a symbol of the supreme sacrifice of Jesus Christ, the basis of their faith.

Many primitive peoples, full of fear and ignorance, grasped at some symbol to drive away their fear of evil and bad luck, and chose the dog to protect them against the demons of the unknown. They did not always actually worship the dog or regard him as a god, although this was sometimes the case. Occasionally the dog is considered a sign of ill fortune or devastation, but nearly always as a token or talisman of good.

Just as black cats have more significance generally than any other color, so color has some importance to the protective qualities of the dog. Nearly always, the most lucky, fortunate or powerful kind of dog is the white one. In China, and Japan too, color was very important. The blood of a white dog smeared around the gates and doors was said to keep away disaster. The Iroquois Indians had a great festival during which a white dog of marvelous temperament and ability was sacrificed to the Great Spirit as a

symbol of their loyalty. In Japan there was a belief that the hair of a white dog could cure illness.

The Chinese, too, always made a great point of the importance of color in a dog. The five-colored dog, featured several times in superstition and legend, symbolized powerful qualities. The patterns on the royal dogs had great importance, and if a puppy was born with a white blaze on the forehead this was highly valued as one of Buddha's thirty-two superior marks. In fact, much of the breeding of the pet dogs of the Imperial court was aimed at including some identifying links such as this with Buddha.

In contrast to the good qualities of the white dog and the sought-after markings on patterned dogs, the black frequently bodes only ill, particularly in European witchcraft. In Wales, the appearance of a black dog near the house of a person who was dying meant that the soul of that person was damned forever, whereas a white dog meant a soul saved. On the other hand, many times in primitive beliefs, a black dog had to be sacrificed to ward off bad luck, such as disease, drought and other disasters. Perhaps this was with the idea that the evil in the black dog had to be offered up before the deity, probably a

The History of the Rottweiler

fearsome one, would be appeased. This is in reverse to the usual practice, in which only the best and finest is considered fit enough to be sacrificed.

Dogs, alas, were often used in ritual sacrifice. The Huron Indians dedicated dogs to the war god so that he would support them in their battles. Other Indian tribes ate dog flesh before going to war, in the belief that the dog's courage would pass into them. Frequently this pre-battle feasting was done with great ritual; in some cases the bones and remains were carefully buried with the proper rites, quite different from the eating of dog flesh as a delicacy—a habit that was, and still is, common practice in many parts of the world.

Anna Katherine Nicholas, in her "bible" *The Book of the Rottweiler,* wrote a prologue about the history of the Rottweiler. Every other Rottweiler book that I have seen seems to have borrowed from her ideas, so I asked her for permission to use some of her material. After all, I had no background in the history of the breed and just learning a few names of great breeders was rather meaningless to me. Miss Nicholas' *Prologue* seems to suit my needs, so here it is.

The layman is inclined to believe, owing to its name, that the Rottweiler originated in Germany and there are those who will try to tell you that it is descended from the Doberman Pinscher. Neither of these theories is fact. History tells us that, although the Rottweiler as we know the breed today is a product of Germany, the origin of the breed actually was in the Ancient Roman Empire.

Behind our modern Rottweiler stands a type of short coated or bristle coated herding dogs known in Ancient Rome. Today's Rottweiler bears a strong resemblance to this early ancestor; the dogs, through the ages have shown only moderate changes in general appearance. The progenitors of the Rottweiler were reliable drover dogs, sometimes used as war dogs in battle, and we have read that the Emperor Nero always kept a number of them around his palace to discourage intruders.

The drover dogs behind the Rottweiler breed served an important function in accompanying Roman troops during their invasions of other European countries. First of all, they were needed for their proficiency at herding, for how else but "on the hoof" could food be

The History of the Rottweiler

transported for the troops in those pre-refrigeration and pre-food preservative days? A large herd for extended invasions was essential, and to guard the herd and prevent loss, so was the drover dog. These dogs probably performed other useful duties, too, on their travels across the European continent. Undoubtedly theirs was a role of major importance in the success of these forays, due to their intelligence, stamina and powerful strength.

Through the St. Gothard Pass over the Alps and into Southern Germany came the invaders with their dogs, into the Wurttemberg area where Rottweill is located. The city itself is the seat of the district bearing this same name; it stands on a hill on the left bank of the Neckar River, centrally located in this lush agricultural area. It is said that Rottweil was so named around the period of 700 A.D., at the time that a Christian Church was erected where formerly had been Roman baths. During the excavation, red tiles of an earlier Roman villa were unearthed, and soon the area became known as "das Rote Wil" or "the red tile."

Some of the drover dogs and their offspring remained in this area when the troops moved on. Owing to its

18

19

22

23

24

The History of the Rottweiler

central location, Rottweil became an important trading center and marketplace to which farmers and cattlemen brought produce for sale. Here again, strong intelligent working dogs of stamina and good "lasting ability" were needed not only to transport the cattle, which sometimes travelled considerable distances, but for the protection of the traders themselves. On the return journey, their moneybags were far safer tied to the collar of a formidable dog than in their own hands should thieves be encountered on these lonely trails.

The butchers, farmers, and cattle dealers came in steadily increasing numbers to the Rottweil area as its popularity as a trading center flourished and cultural interests increased. Visitors, as well as those native to the area, noticed the merits of the "butcher dogs" and the practice began to purposely breed them to improve and increase their type.

Soon a brisk trade developed with people anxious to purchase these fine animals to take home. In respect for their superiority over other types of local dogs, the Roman drover dogs were given the name "Rottweiler," to associate them forever with the area in which they had been so well accepted and appreciated. Thus it is that the descendants of the original Roman drover dogs, as the Germans bred and developed them, we now know as the Rottweiler.

Very quickly a competitive spirit was aroused among owners of these Rottweilers as to who might possess the best and finest dogs, and even as to-day an especially outstanding one in looks, temperament and working ability could bring a sizeable price. One of their attributes as herding dogs has always been their ability to work calmly and without excitement, avoiding any disturbance of the cattle or disquieting behavior as they firmly keep the herd moving along together.

Another job the breed handled well was pulling a cart. Despite all their attributes, however, a time came when the new railroads and resulting regulations resulted in a different form of cattle transportation, and the job of pulling milk carts was switched to donkeys instead of the dogs, thereby depriving the Rottweiler dogs of their two principal forms of usefulness. Happily there were some loyal owners who retained their dogs as guards for their homes and property.

A great surge of renewed interest in the breed began in Northern

The History of the Rottweiler

Germany rather than in their original "home area" (we understand that in 1905 there was only one Rottweiler bitch to be found in all of Rottweil). This took place early in the twentieth century because the breed at that time had been "discovered" for police work. The amusing story we have heard of how this began has to do with a brawl one night in a waterfront saloon in Hamburg. Fourteen very drunken sailors were carrying on a dispute over the favors of a member of the opposite sex. A passing policeman who was a Rottweiler owner was out walking with his dog, came upon the scene and felt that he should take some action. Of course he immediately became the target of the mob, and the Rottweiler was the hero of the situation; in almost no time at all several of the sailors were thrown to the ground and the others were beating a hasty retreat.

It is interesting to find descriptions of the early Rottweilers as they developed in Germany prior to the twentieth century. In general conformation and head shape there is said to have been little change: the massive substance, aura of power, and assured self-confidence has been present right along. A working man rather than a dandy!

Two separate strains were being developed in those days, we gather from our research: the bigger, more muscular dogs for work with the carts; the smaller, more agile and less bulky were deemed more suitable for herding. This difference was due to three considerations: the largest dogs were perhaps too heavily built for lasting stamina on the road; their extra weight might cause accidents in jumping; and their additional height could cause a tendency to nip the cattle in the shoulder or buttocks rather than on the hock as they herded resulting in damaged stock which would bring down its value.

The two size categories were bred as separate strains. Performance alone was sought in the smaller dogs with little concern about their looks. In fact it was in this strain that the "off" coloring by present Standards existed, dogs with white collars, white chests, white spots or feet, or even red dogs with black stripes down their back, or light colored markings were known and accepted, while the larger strain was always scrupulously correct in color as we know it to-day.

Breed Standard for Perfection

A Standard of Perfection is the guide by which we evaluate and judge members of a specific breed of dog. Based on the accepted Standard from the country of the breed's origin, these Standards are drawn up by a parent club for each breed, usually by a committee of experienced authorities selected for their knowledge and willing to undertake the task. Their work next is discussed, reviewed and eventually approved by the Board of Directors and general membership of the specialty club, then submitted to the American Kennel Club for final review, examination and eventual acceptance as the Standard for that breed. As the years pass, sometimes it is found desirable to review and revise or clarify a Standard in order for it to better serve its purpose. That is what has happened to the original Rottweiler Standard which has been in use here since 1935. Although it was a good one as far as it went, it seemed to be in need of expansion to make it more in line with the original Rottweiler Standards from Europe, those of the German Rottweiler club (ADRK) and the Federation Cynologique Internationale (FCI). The following is the 1979 revision of the original American Kennel Club approved Rottweiler Standard. We feel that the revision has been a job well done.

General Appearance: The ideal Rottweiler is a large, robust and powerful dog, black with clearly defined rust markings. His compact build denotes great strength, agility and endurance. Males are characteristically larger, heavier boned and more masculine in appearance.

Size: Males, 24" to 27". Females 22" to 25". Proportion should always be considered rather than height alone. The length of the body, from the breast bone (Sternum) to the rear edge of the pelvis (Ischium) is slightly longer than the height of the dog at the withers; the most desirable proportion being as 10 to 9. Depth of chest should be fifty per cent of the height.

Serious Faults: Lack of proportion, undersize, oversize.

Head: Of medium length, broad between the ears; forehead line seen in profile is moderately arched.

Breed Standard for Perfection

Cheekbones and stop well developed; length of muzzle should not exceed distance between stop and occiput. Skull is preferred dry; however, some wrinkling may occur when dog is alert.

Muzzle: Bridge is straight, broad at base with slight tapering towards tip. Nose is broad rather than round, with black nostrils.

Lips: Always black; corners tightly closed. Inner mouth pigment is dark. A pink mouth is to be penalized.

Teeth: 42 in number (20 upper and 22 lower); strong, correctly placed, meeting in a scissors bite, lower incisors touching inside of upper incisors.

Serious Faults: Any missing tooth, level bite.

Disqualifications: Undershot, overshot, four or more missing teeth.

Eyes: Of medium size, moderately deep set, almond shaped with well fitting lids. Iris of uniform color, from medium to dark brown, the darker shade always preferred.

Serious Faults: Yellow (bird of prey) eyes; eyes not of same color; eyes unequal in size or shape. Hairless lid.

Ears: Pendant, proportionately small, triangular in shape; set well apart and placed on skull so as to make it appear broader when the dog is alert. Ear terminates at approximate mid-cheek level. Correctly held, the inner edge will lie tightly against cheek.

Neck: Powerful, well muscled, moderately long with slight arch and without loose skin.

Body: Topline is firm and level, extending in straight line from withers to croup.

Brisket: Deep, reaching to elbow.

Chest: Roomy, broad with well pronounced forechest.

Ribs: Well sprung.

Loin: Short, deep and well muscled.

Croup: Broad, medium length, slightly sloping.

Breed Standard for Perfection

Tail: Normally carried in horizontal position, giving an impression of an elongation of top line. Carried slightly above horizontal when dog is excited. Some dogs are born without a tail, or a very short stub. Tail is normally docked short close to the body. The set of the tail is more important than length.

Forequarters: Shoulder blade long, well laid back at 45 degree angle. Elbows tight, well under body. Distance from withers to elbow and elbow to ground is equal.

Legs: Strongly developed with straight heavy bone. Not set closely together.

Pasterns: Strong, springy and almost perpendicular to ground.

Feet: Round, compact, well arched toes, turning neither in nor out. Pads thick and hard; nails short, strong and black. Dewclaws may be removed.

Hindquarters: Angulation of hindquarters balances that of forequarters.

Upper Thigh: Fairly long, broad and well muscled.

Stifle Joint: Moderately angulated.

Lower Thigh: Long, powerful, extensively muscled leading into a strong hock joint; metatarsus nearly perpendicular to ground. Viewed from rear, hind legs are straight and wide enough apart to fit in with a properly built body.

Feet: Somewhat longer than front feet, well arched toes turning neither in nor out. Dewclaws must be removed if present.

Coat: Outer coat is straight, coarse, dense, medium length, lying flat. Undercoat must be present on neck and thighs, but should not show through the outer coat. The Rottweiler should be exhibited in a natural condition without trimming, except to remove whiskers if desired.

Fault: Wavy coat.

Disqualification: Long coat.

Color: Always black with rust to mahogany markings. The borderline between black and rust should be clearly defined. The markings should be located as follows: a spot over each eye; on cheeks, as a strip

Breed Standard for Perfection

around each side of the muzzle, but not on the bridge of nose; on throat; triangular mark on either side of breastbone; on forelegs from carpus downward to toes; on inside of rear legs showing down the front of stifle and broadening out in front of rear legs from hock to toes, but not completely eliminating black from back of legs; under tail. Black penciling markings on toes. The undercoat is gray or black.

Quantity and location of rust markings is important and should not exceed ten percent of body color. Insufficient or excessive markings should be penalized.

Serious Faults: Excessive markings; white markings any place on dog (a few white hairs do not constitute a marking); light colored markings.

Disqualifications: Any base color other than black; total absence of markings.

It takes a very practiced eye to be able to judge puppies' conformation show potential with any degree of accuracy. But regardless of how an individual Rottweiler puppy conforms to the breed standard in appearance, it remains a wonderful companion nonetheless.

Breed Standard for Perfection

Gait: The Rottweiler is a trotter. The motion is harmonious, sure, powerful and unhindered, with a strong fore-reach and a powerful rear drive. Front and rear legs are thrown neither in nor out, as the imprint of hindfeet should touch that of forefeet. In a trot, the forequarters and hindquarters are mutually co-ordinated while the back remains firm; as speed is increased legs will converge under body towards a center line.

Character: The Rottweiler should possess a fearless expression with a self-assured aloofness that does not lend itself to immediate and indiscriminate friendships. He has an inherent desire to protect home and family, and is an intelligent dog of extreme hardness and adaptability with a strong willingness to work.

A judge shall dismiss from the ring any shy or vicious Rottweiler.

Shyness: A dog shall be judged fundamentally shy if, refusing to stand for examination it shrinks away from the judge; if it fears an approach from the rear; if it shies at sudden or unusual noises to a marked degree.

Viciousness: A dog that attacks or attempts to attack either the judge or the handler is definitely vicious. An aggressive or belligerent attitude towards other dogs shall not be deemed viciousness.

Faults: The foregoing is a description of the ideal Rottweiler. Any structural fault that detracts from the above-described working dog must be penalized to the extent of the deviation.

Disqualifications: Undershot, overshot, four or more missing teeth. Long coat. Any base color other than black. Total absence of markings.

Your New Puppy

Quite simply, I bought my Rottweiler after reading books about different breeds of dog. The book that "sold" me was Anna Katherine Nicholas' *The Book of the Rottweiler*. What a magnificent book for a magnificent breed!

The dog I was looking for had to have several special attributes. It had to be gentle and very loyal to its owners, get along with younger children pulling and tugging on it, be a watchdog whose bark and size would frighten off juvenile vandals as well as professional thieves, and it had to be a healthy breed without inbred problems due to its conformity. A not-so-important consideration, but an extra, was the ease with which it could adapt to life indoors or outdoors, and the lack of necessity for grooming. The dog that fit this description was the Rottweiler.

Where To Buy It

Wanting a Rottweiler and finding the right one was a chore. The first thing I did was visit my local petshop. Since it was a small town shop, it didn't carry dogs of stature and good breeding, but they suggested that I give them a week to find some good puppies and then I could visit the breeders. I liked this arrangement for then I could have the knowledge of the dog's ancestry by seeing at least its mother, and I could judge from the mother's temperament what kind of dog her puppy might turn out to be. Add to this the fact that I was buying it through a petshop who had a business license and a reputation to worry about, and I felt I had the best of both worlds. My petshop did set up about five visits for me and I selected the puppy that suited me best.

How To Buy It

What I looked for was not body conformation; I was not interested in showing my dog. I just wanted a great companion, protector and friend for the children. I decided to buy the friendliest puppy I could find. Taking the children with me was a great idea. I let them play with the litter until either the puppies got bored or the children got bored. When we met Kaiser (the name we gave him) we knew this was the dog for us. He didn't run and jump onto the children. He came close to each, sniffed and smelled them (by this time they must have had some very interesting doggie odors), then, looking into their faces, his little stub of a tail began to wriggle. As he grew, he kept this same conservative attitude. He became a great watchdog and was absolutely everything we desired in an animal that was to share our home and our lives. I'm so happy that we made the decision to get a Rottweiler . . . and Kaiser in particular.

Our petshop-breeder route was a wise decision, too. The petshop was able to introduce us to his veterinarian who certified to the dog's health *before* we bought him, and the petshop sold us the food, Nylabones, collars and lead that we needed to get started properly.

Sex and Age

This is no place to undertake a "battle of the sexes." Since no dog should run loose, a female, during the brief sex-vulnerable intervals of estrus twice a year, will be chaperoned whenever outdoors; or it is relatively easy to keep her safely confined or to board her with your veterinarian or at a reliable kennel. On the other hand, a male, after he reaches an age to lift his leg, must be let or taken outside to relieve himself four times every single day, no matter what the inconvenience.

No one can make this decision for you. "You pays your money, and takes your choice!"

As to age, two and a half to three months is young enough. By that age, a puppy is weaned and independent of his mother's care and company, day or night. He is well adapted to his diet and a convenient meal schedule. He is old enough for vaccinations against distemper and other contagious diseases (in fact, a vaccination program may have already been started for the puppy by his seller), and he is at the most responsive age to begin to understand and heed the lessons of housebreaking. A younger puppy requires frequent attention, almost foster-mothering, which cannot be delegated to children or neglected even for a few hours. A lower price at a lower age is no bargain.

Selection

When you do pick out a puppy as a pet, don't be hasty; the longer you study puppies, the better you will understand them. Make it your transcendent concern to select only one that radiates good health and spirit and is lively on his feet, whose eyes are bright, whose coat shines, and who comes forward eagerly to make and to cultivate your acquaintance. Don't fall for any shy little darling that wants to retreat to his bed or his box, or plays coy behind other puppies or people, or hides his head under your arm or jacket appealing to your protective instinct. *Pick the puppy who forthrightly picks you! The feeling of attraction should be mutual!*

Documents

Now, a little paper work is in order. When you purchase a purebred puppy, you should receive a transfer of ownership, registration material, and other "papers" (a list of the immunization shots, if any, the puppy may have been given; a note on whether or not the puppy has been wormed; a diet and feeding schedule to which the puppy is accustomed) and you are welcomed as a fellow owner to a long, pleasant association with a most lovable pet, and more (news)paper work.

General Preparation

You have chosen to own a particular puppy. You have chosen it very carefully over all other breeds and all other puppies. So before you ever get that puppy home, you will have prepared for its arrival by reading everything you can get your hands on having to do with the management of dogs and puppies. True, you will run into many conflicting opinions, but at least you will not be starting "blind." Read, study, digest. Talk over your plans with your veterinarian, other "dog people," and the seller of your puppy.

When you get your puppy, you will find that your reading and study are far from finished. You've just scratched the surface in your plan to provide the greatest possible comfort and health for your puppy; and, by the same token, you do want to assure yourself of the greatest possible enjoyment of this wonderful creature. You must be ready for the puppy mentally as well as in the physical requirements.

Transportation

If you take the puppy home by car, protect him from drafts, particularly in cold weather. Wrapped in a towel and carried in the arms or lap of a passenger, the puppy usually will make the trip without mishap. If the pup starts to

Your New Puppy

drool and to squirm, stop the car for a few minutes. Have newspapers handy in case of car-sickness. A covered carton lined with newspapers provides protection for puppy and car, if you are driving alone. Avoid excitement and unnecessary handling of the puppy on arrival. A puppy is a very small "package" to be making complete change of surroundings and company, and he needs frequent rest and refreshment to renew his vitality.

The First Day and Night

When your puppy arrives in your home, put him down on the floor and don't pick him up again, except when it is absolutely necessary. He is a dog, a real dog, and must not be lugged around like a rag doll. Handle him as little as possible, and permit no one to pick him up and baby him. To repeat, *put your puppy on the floor or the ground and let him stay there except when it may be necessary to do otherwise.*

Quite possibly your puppy will be afraid for a while in his new surroundings, without his mother and littermates. Comfort him and reassure him, but don't console him. Don't give him the "oh-you-poor-ittsy-bitsy-puppy" treatment. Be calm, friendly, and reassuring. Encourage him to walk around and sniff over his new home. If it's dark, put on the lights. Let him roam for a few minutes while you and everybody else concerned sit quietly or go about your routine business. Let the puppy come back to you.

Playmates may cause an immediate problem if the new puppy is to be greeted by children or other pets. If not, you can skip this subject. The natural affinity between puppies and children calls for some supervision until a live-and-let-live relationship is established. This applies particularly to a Christmas puppy, when there is more excitement than usual and more chance for a puppy to swallow something upsetting. It is a better plan to welcome the puppy several days before or after the holiday week. Like a baby, your puppy needs much rest and should not be over-handled. Once a child realizes that a puppy has "feelings" similar to his own, and can readily be hurt or injured, the opportunities for play and responsibilities provide exercise and training for both.

For his first night with you, he should be put where he is to sleep every night—say the kitchen, since its floor can usually be easily

Your New Puppy

cleaned. Let him explore the kitchen to his heart's content; close doors to confine him there. Prepare his food and feed him lightly the first night. Give him a pan with some water in it—not a lot, since most puppies will try to drink the whole pan dry. Give him an old coat or a shirt to lie on. Since a coat or shirt will be strong in human scent, he will pick it out to lie on, thus furthering his feeling of security in the room where he has just been fed.

Housebreaking Helps

Now, sooner or later—mostly sooner—your new puppy is going to "puddle" on the floor. First take a newspaper and lay it on the puddle until the urine is soaked up onto the paper. *Save this paper.* Now take a cloth with soap and water, wipe up the floor and dry it well. Then take the wet paper and place it on a fairly large square of newspapers in a convenient corner. When cleaning up, always keep a piece of wet paper on top of the others. Every time he wants to "squat," he will seek out this spot and use the papers. (This routine is rarely necessary for more than three days.) Now leave your puppy for the night. Quite probably he will cry and howl a bit; some are more stubborn than others on this matter. But let him stay alone for the night. This may seem harsh treatment, but it is the best procedure in the long run. Just let him cry; he will weary of it sooner or later.

Beat Him to the Draw

Puppies, like human infants, wake up at the crack of dawn. So, bright and early, your first job is to take him outdoors for a "business trip." Try to keep him out until he has relieved himself. Then give him his first meal of the day, after which you take him out again. Puppies usually want to relieve themselves first thing in the morning, last thing at night, after each feeding, and after each nap. To cut down on "mistakes," take him out often for the first few days, until he learns what he is going out for—and keep him near his newspapers. Caution: Do not force him to rely too much on the newspapers or he will get to the point where he will stay out for hours without doing anything and then rush to the papers when he at last is brought indoors.

Housebreaking is a simple thing if done properly. Just cooperate with the inevitable! Anticipate his need

Your New Puppy

before he does. And for the first few mistakes, say nothing to him—especially the first 24 hours. Then, when he misbehaves, point to the error and quietly but firmly say "No" or "Fooey!" Make it decisive. He must know he has done wrong, but he must *not* be scared to death. And under no circumstance must he be slapped, yelled at, or stamped at. Just a brisk "Fooey" or "No." Work things in such a way that he doesn't get a chance to misbehave.

Collar and Leash Training

Now as to general management, immediately put on him a small leather collar and have a leash to go with it. He probably won't notice the collar at all; but if he does, and seems to fight it, let him fight it and pay no attention. He'll get used to it quickly. Leave it on all the time. Whenever he goes outside, snap a leash onto the collar. City or country, always take your dog out with collar and leash. This is his first taste of discipline. And discipline is not punishment—it is training!

All training is done on the leash. He may buck and plunge a bit at first, finding himself unable to run around at will. Hold the leash

firmly, but let it "give" a lot for the first few days. Do not start him off with the chain collar. Such a collar is ideal later, but it is painful and even dangerous on a young puppy. Gradually teach him to walk quietly on the leash, always on your left side. Hold the leash in such a way to prevent him from running ahead of you or crossing your path. By all means, start his leash- and-collar work as soon as you get him. Don't start his formal training until he is five or six months old, or maybe a little older, depending on the dog himself. Meanwhile, he is learning what "No" means, and he is learning to come when called. Always speak his name first, followed by the command "Come." And make it a command, but slap your knees to encourage him at first. Study your training book now, even though you won't start regular training for months.

Riding in the Car

Start your puppy off right in the car. He will probably have to be boosted in the first few times. Let him sit on the floor. Take him only on short trips for awhile. If the excitement or motion of riding makes him sick, he will begin to drool heavily. When you see this, stop the car and take him out. Let him walk around on the leash a bit—say five or ten minutes. Then put him back in the car and start off again. For several weeks, go for short trips only and make the trips frequent. The younger the puppy, usually the sooner he learns to like driving and the less he is concerned with it.

Take your puppy everywhere—streets, stores—everywhere. Do it in easy stages, but get him accustomed to all sorts of strange sights, sounds, and smells. Thus, when he is mature, he will go anywhere with perfect poise.

Encourage him, too, to stand quietly and be patted by strangers. Be careful that he doesn't learn to dislike children, as sometimes happens with dogs of all breeds, because of rough handling on the part of the children. Let one or two children take him for a walk on his leash once in a while. Let them feed him some special treat as they take him out.

Introducing New Situations

In general, either lead your puppy or encourage him to take the initiative in all new situations. Don't ever "push" him into them. You will get nowhere and may end up spoiling the dog.

With you and your family, observe the same procedures. Let the dog make the move. Encourage him to sit or lie quietly with the family. Let the dog develop into a sensible, normal dog. Don't fuss with him constantly.

Do not misunderstand the instruction not to make a fuss over the puppy. This does not mean you should bring up your dog in a harsh, strict manner. A dog has a limitless reservoir of love and affection and devotion for those he knows and loves. Sure, play with him. Sure, roughhouse with him, but don't make an addlepated ninny out of him by constantly fooling or talking with him. If there is anything worse than a spoiled child, it's a spoiled dog. Both are a pain in the neck to all concerned. So bring up your puppy to be a friendly, well-mannered, happy, healthy dog. If he doesn't "get around," how can he know how to act under all circumstances? So take him around. Start his training early.

To Spay or Not to Spay

To spay a female dog (past tense, *spayed)* is to remove both ovaries from the dog surgically, thus rendering it impossible for the dog ever to have puppies or periods of "heat," or "season." And make no mistake about it, this is major surgery to be performed only by a graduate, licensed veterinarian. However, in his hands, the practice of spaying is quite generally used and is considered a routine operation. The risk involved is almost zero, assuming that the dog is of correct age and is in excellent health and condition.

Needless to say, there is considerable difference of opinion on spaying. "Spay and spoil your female" is the contention of those who are opposed, although just how the female is "spoiled" is not readily apparent. The opponents will tell you that the spayed female becomes sluggish, dull, has no pep or joy in life, gets enormously fat, and wants only to eat and sleep. It is further alleged that the spayed female is rendered stupid and unable to learn anything.

Now, among old-timers in the dog game, there is a very strong conviction that the female is a far better companion and housedog than the male, and the best housedog and companion is a spayed female. These experienced dog keepers have never seen a fat,

stupid spayed female; and they firmly believe that spaying in no way affects the dog's personality or characteristic joy in living. Granted, there is a tendency to get fat, but this situation is easily regulated by proper feeding.

To anyone not interested in breeding dogs but who wants a fine companion and housedog, the spayed female has no superior. Always beautiful anyway, she is keen, smart, and lively.

Special Care for the Brood Bitch

If your female is to be used as a breeding animal, there are certain topics to be covered in the management of the female during her periods of heat.

The female usually comes in heat for the first time between the ages of seven and 12 months. And allowing for some variations in individual dogs, the female will come in heat roughly twice a year, once in the spring and once in the fall, or thereabouts.

The onset of the heat period is marked by a slight discharge of dark red blood from the vulva, or external genital organ, of the female. With this discharge, odorless to humans, comes a gradual swelling and enlargement of the vulva, along with an increased flow of blood, until the ninth or tenth day, at which time the vulva is quite enlarged and the flow has begun to be pinkish or amber colored. The discharge gradually pales out and decreases during the third week. But while the heat period is usually considered to be three weeks, it is much safer to count it a month in duration.

If you live in the city, the heat period will cause you little if any inconvenience, since, in the city, dogs are more apt to be leashed or more carefully controlled than dogs in the suburbs and country. But the safe rule, to guard against accidental breeding, is to keep your female always on a lead throughout the entire heat period. As for the droplets of discharge around the house, they are odorless and may easily be removed by wiping with a damp cloth.

In the country or suburbs, you may have somewhat of a problem. Again, take your female outside only on a leash and keep her close beside you. If possible, walk her a little way from the house to relieve herself, keeping a sharp lookout for visiting males. Some males are extremely fast operators; and unless you are very careful, especially from the seventh or eighth day on, you may have an unwanted breeding before you know it. In this instance, once such a breeding has begun, there is absolutely nothing you can do about it. Attempted separation of the two animals will result in serious injury to both. However, should you have such bad luck, immediately take your female to your veterinarian. Sometimes he can prevent a litter of mutts.

Indoors, continue your caution. Along about the eleventh or twelfth day, your female may sneak outside if not watched, and she is sure to run into a group of waiting males. Keep her under lock and key for a full month!

Feeding

Now let's talk about feeding your dog, a subject so simple that it's amazing there is so much nonsense and misunderstanding about it. Is it expensive to feed a dog? No, it is not! You can feed your dog economically and keep him in perfect shape the year round, or you can feed him expensively. He'll thrive either way, and let's see why this is true.

First of all, remember a dog is a dog. Dogs do not have a high degree of selectivity in their food, and unless you spoil them with great variety (and possibly turn them into poor, "picky" eaters) they will eat almost anything that they become accustomed to. Many dogs flatly refuse to eat nice, fresh beef. They pick around it and eat everything else. But meat—bah! Why? They aren't accustomed to it! They are hounds. They'd eat rabbit fast enough, but they refuse beef because they aren't used to it.

Variety Not Necessary

A good general rule of thumb is forget all about human preferences and don't give a thought to variety. Choose the right diet for your dog and feed it to him day after day, year after year, winter and summer. But what is the right diet?

Hundreds of thousands of dollars have been spent in canine nutrition research. The results are pretty conclusive, so you needn't go into a lot of experimenting with trials of this and that every other week. Research has proven just what your dog needs to eat and to keep healthy.

Dog Food

There are almost as many right diets as there are dog experts, but the basic diet most often recommended is one that consists of a dry food, either meal or kibble form. There are several of these of excellent quality, manufactured by reliable concerns, research tested, and nationally advertised. They are inexpensive, highly satisfactory, and easily available in stores everywhere in containers of five to fifty pounds. Larger amounts cost less per pound, usually.

Feeding

If you have a choice of brands, it is usually safer to choose the better-known one; but even so, carefully read the analysis on the package. Do not choose any food in which the protein level is less than 25 percent, and be sure that this protein comes from both animal *and* vegetable sources. The good dog foods have meat meal, fish meal, liver, and such, plus protein from alfalfa and soybeans, as well as some dried-milk product. Note the vitamin content carefully. See that they are all there in good proportions; and be especially certain that the food contains properly high levels of vitamins A and D, two of the most perishable and important ones. Note the B-complex level, but don't worry about carbohydrate and mineral levels. These substances are plentiful and cheap and not likely to be lacking in a good brand.

The advice given for how to choose a dry food also applies to moist or canned types of dog foods, if you decide to feed one of these.

Having chosen a really good food, feed it to your dog as the manufacturer directs. And once you've started, stick to it. Never change if you can possibly help it. A switch from one meal or kibble-type food can usually be made without too much upset; however, a change will almost invariably give you (and the dog) some trouble.

Fat Important; Meat Optional

While the better dog foods are complete in themselves in every respect, there is one item to add to the food, and that is *fat*—any kind of melted animal fat. It can be lard, bacon, or ham fat or from beef, lamb, pork, or poultry. A grown dog should have at least a tablespoon or two of melted fat added to one feeding a day. If you feed your dog morning and night, give him half of the fat in each feeding.

The addition of meat to this basic ration is optional. There is a sufficient amount of everything your dog needs already in the food, but you may add any meat you wish, say, a half to a quarter of a pound. In adding meat, the glandular meats are best, such as kidneys, pork liver, and veal or beef heart. They are all cheap to buy and are far higher sources of protein than the usual muscle meat humans insist on. Cook these meats slightly or feed them raw. Liver and kidney should be cooked a little and fed sparingly since they are laxative to some dogs. Heart is ideal, raw or cooked. Or you can feed beef, lamb, ocean fish well cooked, and pork.

Feeding

When Supplements Are Needed

Now what about supplements of various kinds, mineral and vitamin, or the various oils? They are all okay to add to your dog's food. However, if you are feeding your dog a correct diet, and this is easy to do, no supplements are necessary unless your dog has been improperly fed, has been sick, or is having puppies. Vitamins and minerals are naturally present in all foods; and to ensure against any loss through processing, they are added in concentrated form to the dog food you use. Except on the advice of your veterinarian, extra and added amounts of vitamins can prove harmful to your dog! The same risk goes with minerals.

Feeding Schedule

When and how much food to give your dog? As to when (except in the instance of puppies which will be taken up later), suit yourself. You may feed two meals per day or the same amount in one single feeding, either morning or night. As to how to prepare the food and how much to give, it is generally best to follow the directions on the food package. Your own dog may want a little more or a little less.

Fresh, cool water should always be available to your dog. This is important to good health throughout his lifetime.

All Dogs Need to Chew

Puppies and young dogs need something with resistance to chew on while their teeth and jaws are developing—for cutting the puppy teeth, to induce growth of the permanent teeth under the puppy teeth, to assist in getting rid of the puppy teeth at the proper time, to help the permanent teeth through the gums, to ensure normal jaw development, and to settle the permanent teeth solidly in the jaws.

The adult dog's desire to chew stems from the instinct for tooth cleaning, gum massage, and jaw exercise—plus the need for an outlet for periodic doggie tensions.

This is why dogs, especially puppies and young dogs, will often destroy property worth hundreds of dollars when their chewing instinct is not diverted from their owner's possessions. And this is why you should provide your dog with something to chew—something that

Feeding

has the necessary functional qualities, is desirable from the dog's viewpoint, and is safe for your dog.

It is very important that dogs not be permitted to chew on anything they can break or on any indigestible thing from which they can bite sizeable chunks. Sharp pieces, such as from a bone which can be broken by a dog, may pierce the intestinal wall and kill. Indigestible things which can be bitten off in chunks, such as from shoes or rubber or plastic toys, may cause an intestinal stoppage (if not regurgitated) and bring painful death, unless surgery is promptly performed.

Strong natural bones, such as 4- to 8-inch lengths of round shin bone from mature beef—either the kind you can get from a butcher or one of the variety available commercially in pet stores—may serve your dog's teething needs if his mouth is large enough to handle them effectively. You may be tempted to give your puppy a smaller bone and he may not be able to break it when you do, but puppies grow rapidly and the power of their jaws constantly increases until maturity. This means that a growing dog may break one of the smaller bones at any time, swallow the pieces, and die painfully before you realize what is wrong.

All hard natural bones are highly abrasive. If your dog is an avid chewer, natural bones may wear away his teeth prematurely; hence, they then should be taken away from your dog when the teething purposes have been served. The badly worn, and usually painful, teeth of many mature dogs can be traced to excessive chewing on natural bones.

Contrary to popular belief, knuckle bones which can be chewed up and swallowed by the dog provide little, if any, useable calcium or other nutriment. They do, however, disturb the digestion of most dogs and cause them to vomit the nourishing food they need.

Dried rawhide products of various types, shapes, sizes, and prices are available on the market and have become quite popular. However, they don't serve the primary chewing functions very well; they are a bit messy when wet from mouthing, and most dogs chew them up rather rapidly—but they have been considered safe for dogs until recently. Now, more and more incidents of death, and near death, by strangulation have been reported to be the result of partially swallowed chunks of rawhide swelling in the throat. More

44

Feeding

recently, some veterinarians have been attributing cases of acute constipation to large pieces of incompletely digested rawhide in the intestine.

The nylon bones, especially those with natural meat and bone fractions added, are probably the most complete, safe, and economical answer to the chewing need. Dogs cannot break them or bite off sizeable chunks; hence, they are

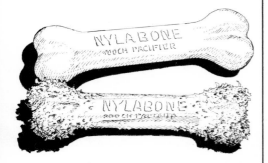

The upper Nylabone has not yet been chewed; the lower Nylabone shows normal signs of wear.

completely safe—and being longer lasting than other things offered for the purpose, they are economical.

Hard chewing raises little bristle-like projections on the surface of the nylon bones—to provide effective interim tooth cleaning and vigorous gum massage, much in the same way your toothbrush does it for you. The little projections are raked off and swallowed in the form of thin shavings, but the chemistry of the nylon is such that they break down in the stomach fluids and pass through without effect.

The toughness of the nylon provides the strong chewing resistance needed for important jaw exercise and effectively aids teething functions, but there is no tooth wear because nylon is non-abrasive. Being inert, nylon does not support the growth of microorganisms; and it can be washed in soap and water or it can be sterilized by boiling or in an autoclave.

Nylabone® is highly recommended by veterinarians as a safe, healthy nylon bone that can't splinter or chip. Nylabone® is frizzled by the dog's chewing action, creating a toothbrush-like surface that cleanses the teeth and massages the gums. Nylabone® and Nylaball® the only chew products made of flavor-impregnated solid nylon, are available in your local pet shop.

Nothing, however, substitutes for periodic professional attention to your dog's teeth and gums, not any more than your toothbrush can do that for you. Have your dog's teeth cleaned by your veterinarian at least once a year (twice a year is better) and he will be healthier, happier, and far more pleasant to live with.

Training

You owe proper training to your dog. The right and privilege of being trained is his birthright; and whether your dog is going to be a handsome, well-mannered housedog and companion, a show dog, or whatever possible use he may be put to, the basic training is always the same—all must start with basic obedience, or what might be called "manners training."

Your dog must come instantly when called and obey the "Sit" or "Down" command just as fast; he must walk quietly at "Heel," whether on or off the lead. He must be mannerly and polite wherever he goes; he must be polite to strangers on the street and in stores. He must be orderly in the presence of other dogs. He must not bark at children on roller skates, motorcycles, or domestic animals. And he must be restrained from chasing cats. It is not a dog's inalienable right to chase cats, and he must be reprimanded for it.

Professional Training

How do you go about this training? Well, it's a very simple procedure, pretty well standardized by now. First, if you can afford the extra expense, you may send your dog to a professional trainer, where in 30 to 60 days he will learn how to be a "good dog." If you enlist the services of a good professional trainer, follow his advice about when to come to see the dog. No, he won't forget you, but too-frequent visits at the wrong time may slow down his training progress. And using a "pro" trainer means you will have to go for some training, too, after the trainer feels your dog is ready to go home. You will have to learn how your dog works, just what to expect of him and how to use what the dog has learned after he is home.

Obedience Training Class

Another way to train your dog (many experienced dog people think this is the best) is to join an obedience-training class right in your own community. There is such a group in nearly every community nowadays. Here you will be working with a group of people who are also just starting out. You will actually be training your own dog, since all work is done under the direction of a head trainer who will make suggestions to you and also tell you when and how to correct your dog's errors. Then, too, working with

Training

such a group, your dog will learn to get along with other dogs. And, what is more important, he will learn to do exactly what he is told to do, no matter how much confusion there is around him or how great the temptation to go his own way.

Write to your national kennel club for the location of a training club or class in your locality. Sign up. Go to it regularly—every session! Go early and leave late! Both you and your dog will benefit tremendously.

Train Him By The Book

The third way of training your dog is by the book. Yes, you can do it this way and do a good job of it too. If you can read and if you're smarter than the dog, you'll do a good job. But in using the book method, select a book, buy it, study it carefully; then study it some more, until the procedures are almost second nature to you. *Then* start your training. But stay with the book and its advice and exercises. Don't start in and then make up a few rules of your own. If you don't follow the book, you'll get into jams you can't get out of by yourself. If after a few hours of short training sessions your dog is

still not working as he should, get back to the book for a study session, because it's *your* fault, not the dog's! The procedures of dog training have been so well systematized that it must be your fault, since literally thousands of fine dogs have been trained by the book.

After your dog is "letter perfect" under all conditions, then, if you wish, go on to advanced training and trick work.

Your dog will love his obedience training, and you'll burst with pride at the finished product! Your dog will enjoy life even more, and you'll enjoy your dog more. And remember—you *owe* good training to your dog!

There are a number of good books that give detailed training information.

Showing

A show dog is a comparatively rare thing. He is one out of several litters of puppies. He happens to be born with a degree of physical perfection that closely approximates the standard by which the breed is judged in the show ring. Such a dog should, at maturity, be able to win or approach his championship in good, fast company at the larger shows. Upon finishing his championship, he is apt to be highly desirable as a breeding animal. As a proven stud, he will automatically command a high price for service.

Showing dogs is a lot of fun—yes, but it is a highly competitive sport. Though all the experts were once beginners, the odds are against a novice. You will be showing against experienced handlers, both pro and amateur, people who have devoted a lifetime to breeding, picking the right ones, and then showing those dogs through to their championships. Moreover, the most perfect dog ever born has faults, and in your hands the faults will be far more evident than with the experienced handler who knows how to minimize his dog's faults. There are but a few points on the sad side of the picture.

The experienced handler, however, was not born knowing the ropes. He learned—*and so can you!* You can if you will put in the same time, study, and keen observation that he did. But it will take time!

Key to Success

First, search for a truly fine show-prospect puppy. Take the puppy home, raise him by the book, and, as carefully as you know how, give him every chance to mature into the dog hoped for. Some dog experts recommend keeping a show-prospect puppy out of big shows, even Puppy Classes, until he is mature. When he is approaching maturity, break him in at match shows (more on these later); after this experience for the dog and you, then go gunning for the big wins at the big shows.

48

Showing

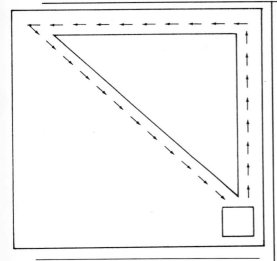

Although there are different patterns to follow when gaiting your dog, this is the one most frequently used.

Next step: read the standard by which the breed is judged. Study it until you know it by heart. Having done this—and while your puppy is at home (where he should be) growing into a fine normal, healthy dog—go to every dog show you can possibly reach. Sit at the ringside and watch the judging. Keep your ears and eyes open. Do your own judging, holding each of those dogs against the standard, which you now know by heart.

In your evaluations, don't start off looking for faults. Look for the virtues—the best qualities. How does a given dog shape up against the standard? Having looked for and noted the virtues, then note the faults and see what prevents a given dog from standing correctly or moving well. Weigh these faults against the virtues, since, ideally, every feature of the dog should contribute to the harmonious whole.

"Ringside Judging"

It's a good practice to make notes on each dog, always holding the dog against the standard. In "ringside judging," forget your personal preference for this or that feature. What does the standard say about it? Watch carefully as the judge places the dogs in a given class. It is difficult from the ringside always to see why number one was placed over the second dog. Try to follow the judge's reasoning. Later try to talk with the judge after he is finished (not every judge will have the time or inclination for this). Ask him questions as to why he placed certain dogs and not others. Listen while the judge explains his placings.

When you're not at the ringside, talk with the fanciers and breeders. Don't be afraid to ask opinions or say that you don't know. You have a lot of listening to do, and it will help you a great deal and speed up

Showing

your personal progress if you are a good listener.

Join the Clubs

You will find it worthwhile to join the national kennel club, which is the governing body for all purebred dogs in a particular country, and to subscribe to its magazine, if one is published. From this national kennel club, you can learn the location of the national breed club (known as the "parent club" for that breed), which you also should join. Being a member of these clubs will afford you the opportunity to get to know other people who share your interests and concerns, to learn more about your breed, and to find out when and where match shows and point shows will be held.

For information regarding sanctioned shows in most English-speaking areas, write to one of the kennel clubs listed below:

American Kennel Club
51 Madison Avenue
New York, NY 10010
USA

Australian Kennel Club
Royal Show Grounds
Ascot Vale, Victoria
Australia

British Kennel Club
1 Clarges Street
London 41Y 8AB
England

Canadian Kennel Club
2150 Bloor Street West
Toronto, Ontario M6S 4V7
Canada

Irish Kennel Club
23 Earlsfort Terrace
Dublin 2
Ireland

Prepare for the Show

The first thing you must do to prepare for a show is to find out the dates and rules of the show you intend to attend. Write to the national kennel club and get a copy of their show dates and rules (and rules for obedience competition or field trials or whatever type of competition you are interested in).

You also must teach your dog and yourself some basics of dog showing. You must learn to "stack" your dog, and your dog must learn to stay in this show stance whenever required to do so. Your dog must learn to accept being examined by a stranger (in other words, the judge at the show). You will have to learn how to gait your dog, and your dog

Showing

must learn how to move properly at your side.

Enter Match Shows

Match shows differ from regular shows only in that no championship points are given. These shows are especially designed to launch young dogs (and young handlers) on a show career.

With the ring deportment you have watched at big shows firmly in mind and practice, enter your dog in as many match shows as you can. When in the ring, you have two jobs. One is to see to it that your dog is always being seen to best advantage. The other job is to keep your eye on the judge to see what he may want you to do next. Watch only the judge and your dog. Be quick and be alert; do exactly as the judge directs. Don't speak to him except to answer his questions. If he does something you don't like, don't say so. And don't irritate the judge (and everybody else) by constantly talking and fussing with your dog.

In moving about the ring, remember to keep clear of dogs beside you or in front of you. Many dog fanciers feel that you should *not*

show your dog in a regular point show until he is at least close to maturity and after both you and he have had time to perfect ring manners and poise in the match shows.

Point Shows

Point shows are for purebred dogs registered with the club that is sanctioning the show. Each dog is entered in the show class which is appropriate for his age, sex, and previous show record. The show classes usually include Puppy, Novice, Bred-by-Exhibitor, American-bred, and Open; and there may also be a Veterans Class and Brace and Team Classes, among others.

There also may be a Junior Showmanship Class, a competition for youngsters. Young people between the ages of 10 and 16, inclusively, compete to see who best handles their dog, rather than to see which dog is best, as is done in the other classes.

For a complete discussion of show dogs, dog shows, and showing a dog, read *Successful Dog Show Exhibiting* by Anna Katherine Nicholas (T.F.H. Publications, Inc.).

Breeding

So you have a female dog and you want to breed her for a litter of puppies. Wonderful idea—very simple—lots of fun—make a lot of money. Well, it *is* a wonderful idea, but stop right there. It's not very simple—and you won't make a lot of money. Having a litter of puppies to bring up is

The external skeletal parts of a dog: 1. Cranium. 2. Cervical vertebra. 3. Thoracic vertebra. 4. Rib. 5. Lumber vertebra. 6. Ilium. 7. Femur. 8. Fibula. 9. Tibia. 10. Tarsus. 11. Metatarsus. 12. Phalanges. 13. Phalanges. 14. Ulna. 15. Radius. 16. Humerus. 17. Scapula.

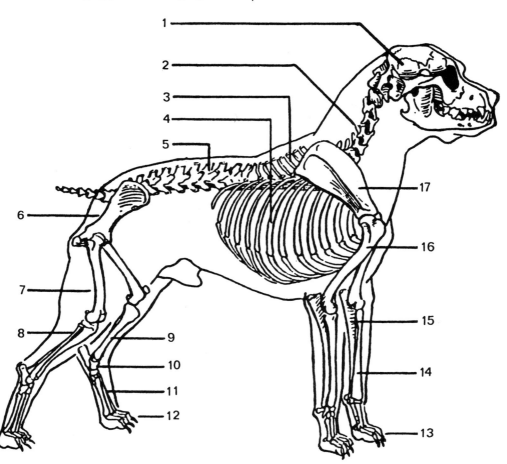

Breeding

hard, painstaking, thoughtful work; and only a few people regard such work as fun.

Breed Better Dogs

Bear in mind this very important point: Being a dog breeder is not just breeding dear Tillie to that darned good-looking male down the street. Would that it were that simple! Such a breeding will undoubtedly produce puppies. But that is not all you want. When you breed your female, it is only after the most careful planning—with every effort being made to be sure that the resulting puppies will be even better than the parent dogs (that they will come even closer to the standard than the parent animals) and that all the puppies will have good homes. Any fool can breed a litter of puppies; but only a careful, thoughtful, intelligent person can breed a litter of better puppies of your breed of dog. That must be your goal in breeding!

You can become a good novice breeder if you truly love the breed and are seriously concerned with the past, present, and future of the breed. You will breed your female only according to established scientific principles. Your personal sentiments have no place in the careful planning that goes on before you actually breed your female. The science of mammalian genetics is not a precise science like, say, mathematics. And the extensive reading you will do on the science (or art) of breeding dogs before you start to choose a stud will give you some idea of the variable factors you will be dealing with. It is a vast subject; but with the few brief pointers given here and additional reading and study, you can at least start on the right track.

Plan It on Paper

The principles of animal breeding are the same, whether the subjects be beef cattle, poultry, or dogs. To quote a cattle breeder, every breeding is first made "on paper" and later in the barnyard. In other words, first the blood strains of the animals are considered as to what goes well with what, so far as recorded ancestry is concerned. Having worked this out, the two animals to be mated must be studied and compared. If one does not excel where the other is lacking, at least in most points, then the paper planning must start over again and different animals be considered.

Breeding

With your own dog, there are several "musts" that are really axioms. First, breed only the best to the best. Two inferior animals will produce nothing but inferior animals, as surely as night follows day. To breed an inferior dog to another inferior one is a crime against the breed. So start by breeding the best to the best. And here again, an accurate knowledge of the standard is essential to know just what is best.

"Compensation" Breeding

No perfect dog has yet been whelped. Your female may be a winning show dog. She may be a champion. But she does have faults. In breeding her to a fine male, you must consider "compensation" breeding. She must compensate for his shortcomings and he for hers. For example, your female may be ideal in most respects but have faulty feet. So the male you choose, however ideal in other respects, *must* have ideal feet, as had his sire and dam too. In this way you may overcome the foot faults in your female's puppies.

This same principle applies to the correction of faults in any section of either male or female. But, you say, my dog has a pedigree as long as your arm. Must be good! Sad but true, a pedigree will not necessarily produce good puppies. A pedigree is no more—and no less—than your dog's recorded ancestry. Yes, you must know what dogs are in your dog's pedigree, but the most important point is, Were they good dogs? What were their faults and virtues? And to what degree did these dogs transmit these faults and virtues?

Breeding Methods

Now you may have heard that "like begets like." This is true and it is also false! Likes can beget likes only when both parent animals have the same likeness through generations of both family lines. The only way known to "fix" virtues and to eliminate faults is to mate two dogs of fairly close relationship bloodwise, two dogs which come from generations of likes and are family-related in their likeness. In this way you may ensure a higher and regular percentage of puppies which can be expected to mature into adults free at least from major faults under the standard. The likes must have the same genetic inheritance.

Through this "family" breeding, or line-breeding, correct type is set

Care of Mother and Family

and maintained. If both family lines are sound to begin with, family breeding and even close inbreeding (mating closely related dogs such as father and daughter) will merely improve the strain—but only in skilled hands. "Outcrossing" is mating dogs of completely different bloodlines with no, or only a few, common ancestors; it is used when undesirable traits begin to haunt closer breeding or when the breeder wants to bring in a specific trait or feature. The finest dogs today are the result of just such breeding methods. Study, expert advice, and experience will enable you, a novice, to follow these principles. So in your planning, forget the old nonsense about idiots and two-headed monsters coming from closely related parents.

Then, too, in your planning and reading, remember that intangible virtues, as well as physical ones, are without doubt inherited, as are faults in those intangibles. For example, in breeding bird dogs, where "nose sense" is of greatest importance, this factor can to a degree be fixed for future generations of puppies when the ancestors on both sides have the virtue of "nose sense." Just so, other characteristics of disposition or temperament can be fixed.

Let us assume that you have selected the right stud dog for your female and that she has been bred. In some 58 to 63 days, you will be presented with a nice litter of puppies. But there are a number of things to be gone over and prepared for in advance of the whelping date.

Before your female was bred, she was, of course, checked by your veterinarian and found to be in good condition and free from worms of any sort. She was in good weight but not fat. Once your female has been bred, you should keep your veterinarian informed of your female's progress; and when the whelping is imminent, your vet should be informed so that he can be on call in case any problems arise.

There's an old saying, "A litter should be fed from the day the bitch is bred," and there is a world of truth in it. So from the day your female is bred right up to the time the puppies are fully weaned, the mother's food is of the greatest importance. Puppies develop very rapidly in their 58 to 63 days of gestation, and their demands on the mother's system for nourishment are great. In effect, you are feeding your female and one to six or more other dogs, all at the same time.

Care of Mother and Family

The color captions for pages 57-64 can be found on page 16.

Additions to Regular Diet

For the first 21 days, your female will need but few additions to her regular diet. Feed her as usual, except for the addition of a small amount of "pot " or cottage cheese. This cheese, made from sour milk, is an ideal, natural source of added protein, calcium, and phosphorus—all essential to the proper growth of the unborn litter. Commercial vitamin-mineral supplements are unnecessary if the mother is fed the proper selection of natural foods.

Most commercial supplements are absolutely loaded with mineral calcium. You will usually find that the bulk of the contents is just plain calcium, a cheap and plentiful substance. Some dog experts believe, however, that calcium from an animal source like cheese is far more readily assimilated, and it is much cheaper besides. At any rate, do not use a commercial supplement without consulting your veterinarian and telling him the diet your dog is already getting.

Increase Food Intake

Along about the fifth week, the litter will begin to show a little, and now is the time to start an increase in food intake, not so much in bulk as in nutritive value. The protein content of your female's regular diet should be increased by the addition of milk products (cottage cheese, for example) meat (cooked pork liver, raw beef or veal heart, or some other meat high in protein), and eggs (either the raw yolk alone or, if the white is used, the egg should be cooked). Meanwhile, high-calorie foods should be decreased. The meat, cut into small pieces or ground, can be added to the basic ration. Mineral and vitamin supplements and cod-liver oil or additional fat also can be given to the female at this point, if your veterinarian so recommends.

Feed Several Times A Day

By now, your female is but a few weeks away from her whelping date, and the growing puppies are compressing her internal organs to an uncomfortable degree. She will have to relieve herself with greater frequency now. The stomach, too, is being compressed, so try reducing

BEST OF BREED
OR VARIETY
HENDERSONVILLE
KENNEL CLUB
APRIL 1982
PHOTO BY SABRINA

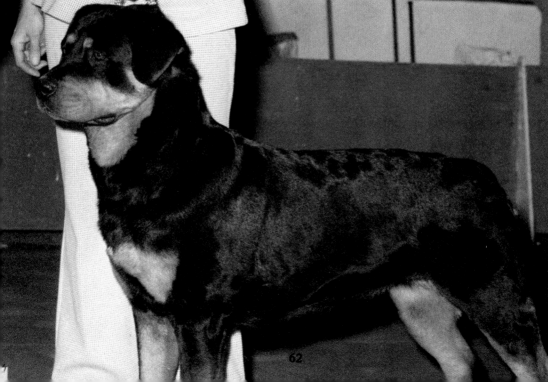

Care of Mother and Family

the basic ration slightly and at the same time increasing the meats, eggs, and milk products. Feed several small meals per day in order to get in the proper, stepped-up quantity of food without causing the increased pressure of a single large meal. The bitch should be fed generously, but she should not be allowed to become overweight.

Regular Exercise Important

A great deal of advice has been given by experts on keeping the female quiet from the day she is bred all through the pregnancy. Such quiet, however, is not natural and it cannot be enforced. Naturally, the female should not be permitted to go in for fence jumping; but she will be as active as ever during the first few weeks and gradually she will, of her own accord, slow down appropriately, since no one knows quite as much about having puppies as the dog herself—up to a point. But see to it that your female has plenty of gentle exercise all along. She'll let you know when she wants to slow down.

The color captions for pages 57-64 can be found on page 16.

Treat her normally, and don't let her be the victim of all the sentimentality that humans with impending families are heir to.

Whelping Imminent

About the morning of the 58th day or shortly thereafter, your female, who now looks like an outsize beer barrel, will suddenly refuse her food. She may drink water, however. If you have been observant as things progressed, your hand, if not your eye, will tell you that the litter has dropped. The female now has a saggy abdomen, and this is the tip-off that whelping will occur soon, usually well within the next 24 hours. As the actual whelping hour approaches, the mother will become increasingly restless. She will seek out dark places like closets. She will scratch at the floor and wad up rugs as if making a bed. She is pretty miserable right now, so be gently sympathetic with her but *not maudlin!*

Get her to stay in the whelping box you have had prepared for several days. The floor of the box should be covered with an old blanket or towel so that she will feel comfortable there. When the whelping starts, replace the bedding

Care of Mother and Family

with newspapers; these can be replaced as they get scratched up or soiled.

The whelping box should be located in a warm, not hot, place free from drafts. The area should also be fairly quiet. You may, if you wish, confine her to the box by hitching her there with a leash to a hook three or four feet off the floor so she won't get twisted up in it. But when actual whelping starts, take off both leash and collar. Then, get yourself a chair and prepare for an all-night vigil. Somehow puppies always seem to be born at night, and the process is good for 12 to 14 hours usually.

Labor Begins

Stay with her when she starts to whelp, you and one other person she knows well and who is an experienced breeder. No audience, please! A supply of warm water, old turkish towels, and plenty of wiping rags are in order at this point.

When labor commences, the female usually assumes a squatting position, although some prefer to lie down. The first puppy won't look much like a puppy to you when it is fully expelled from the female. It will be wrapped in a dark, membranous sac, which the mother will tear open with her teeth, exposing one small, noisy pup—very wet. Let the mother lick the puppy off and help to dry it. She will also bite off the navel cord. This may make the puppy squeal, but don't worry, mama is not trying to eat her pup. The mother may eat a few of the sacs; this is normal. When she is through cleaning the puppy off, pick up the puppy and gently but firmly give it a good rubbing with a turkish towel. Do this in full sight of the mother and close enough so that she will not leave her whelping box.

When the puppy is good and dry and "squawking" a bit, place it near the mother or in a shallow paper box close to the mother so she can see it but will not step on it when she becomes restless with labor for the second puppy. If the room temperature is lower than 70 degrees, place a hot-water bottle wrapped in a towel near the puppies. Be sure to keep the water changed and warm so the puppies aren't lying on a cold water bottle. Constant warmth is essential.

Most dogs are easy whelpers, so you need not anticipate any trouble. Just stay with the mother, more as an observer than anything else. The experienced breeder who is keeping you company, or your vet, should handle any problems that arise.

Care of Mother and Family

Post-natal Care

When you are reasonably certain that the mother has finished whelping, have your veterinarian administer the proper amount of obstetrical pituitrin. This drug will induce labor again, thus helping to expel any retained afterbirth or dead puppy.

Inspect your puppies carefully. Rarely will any deformities be found; but if there should be any, make a firm decision to have your veterinarian destroy the puppy or puppies showing deformities.

During and after whelping, the female is very much dehydrated, so at frequent intervals she should be offered lukewarm milk or meat soup, slightly thickened with well-soaked regular ration. She will relish liquids and soft foods for about 24 hours, after which she will go back to her regular diet. But be sure she has a constant supply of fresh water available. Feed her and keep her water container outside the whelping box.

After all of the puppies have been born, the mother might like to go outside for a walk. Allow her this exercise. She probably won't want to be away from her puppies more than a minute or two.

The puppies will be blind for about two weeks, with the eyes gradually opening up at that time. The little pups will be quite active and crawl about over a large area. Be sure that all of the puppies are getting enough to eat. If the mother sits or stands, instead of lying still to nurse, the probable cause is scratching from the puppies nails. You can remedy this by clipping them, as you do hers.

Weaning Time

Puppies can usually be completely weaned at six weeks of age, although you can start to feed them at three weeks. They will find it easier to lap semi-solid food. At four weeks they should be given four meals a day, and soon they will do without their mother entirely. Start them on mixed dog food, or leave it with them in a dish for self-feeding. Don't leave water with them all the time; at this age everything is to play with and they will use it as a wading pool. They can drink all they need if it is offered several times a day, after meals.

As the puppies grow up, the mother will go into the box only to nurse them, first sitting up and then standing. The periods of time between the mother's visits to the box will gradually lengthen, until it is no longer necessary for her to nurse the pups.

Health and Disease

First, don't be frightened by the number of health problems that a dog might have over the course of his life-time. The majority of dogs never have any of them. Don't become a dog-hypochondriac. All dogs have days when they feel lazy and want to lie around doing nothing. For the few problems that you might be concerned about, remember that your veterinarian is your dog's best friend. When you first get your puppy, select a veterinarian whom you have faith in. He will get to know your dog and will be glad to have you consult him for advice. A dog needs little medical care, but that little is essential to his good health and well-being. He needs a proper diet given at regular hours; clean, roomy housing; daily exercise; companionship and love; frequent grooming; and regular check-ups by your veterinarian.

Using a Thermometer and Giving Medicines

Almost every serious ailment shows itself by an increase in the dog's body temperature. If your dog acts lifeless, looks dull-eyed, and gives the impression of illness,

The proper way to give a pill or tablet.

check his temperature by using a rectal thermometer made of either plastic or glass. Hold the dog securely, insert the thermometer (which you have lubricated with petroleum jelly), and take a reading. The average normal temperature for your dog will be 101.5 °F. Excitement may raise the temperature slightly; but any rise of

The proper way to give liquid medication.

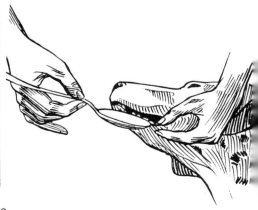

68

Health and Disease

more than a few points is cause for alarm, and your vet should be consulted.

Giving medicines to your dog is not really difficult. In order to administer a liquid medication, do not open the dog's mouth. Instead, form a pocket by pulling out the lower lip at the corner of the mouth; pour the medicine in with a spoon; hold the head only very slightly upward. (If the head is held too high, the medicine may enter the windpipe instead of the passage to the stomach, thus choking the dog.) With agitated animals, medicine can still be given by this method, even though the dog's mouth is held shut with a tape or a muzzle.

In order to administer a pill or tablet, raise your dog's head slightly and open his mouth. (Using one hand, grasp the cheeks of the dog, and then press inward. The pressure of the lips pushed against the teeth will keep the mouth open). With the other hand, place the pill or tablet far back on the middle of the tongue. Quickly remove your hand from the dog's cheeks; hold the dog's mouth closed (but not too tightly), and gently massage his throat. You can tell the medicine has been swallowed when the tip of the dog's tongue shows between his front teeth.

A Vaccination Schedule

Prevention is the key word for many dog diseases, and the best prevention is a series of vaccinations administered by your veterinarian. Such contagious diseases as distemper, hepatitis, parainfluenza, leptospirosis, rabies, and canine parvovirus can be virtually eliminated by strictly following a vaccination schedule.

Distemper is probably the most virulent of all dog diseases. Young dogs are most susceptible to it, although it may affect dogs of all ages. The dog will lose his appetite, seem depressed, feel chilled, and run a fever. Often he will have a watery discharge from his eyes and nose. Unless treated promptly, the disease goes into advanced stages with infections of the lungs, intestines, and nervous system; and dogs that recover may be left with some impairment such as paralysis, convulsions, a twitch, or some other defect, usually spastic in nature. The best protection against this is very early inoculation with a series of permanent shots and a booster shot each year thereafter.

Hepatitis is a viral disease spread by contact. The initial symptoms of drowsiness, vomiting, great thirst, loss of appetite, and a high temperature closely resemble those

69

Health and Disease

of distemper. These symptoms are often accompanied by swellings of the head, neck, and abdomen. The disease strikes quickly; death may occur in just a few hours. Protection is afforded by injection with a vaccine.

Parainfluenza is commonly called "kennel cough." Its main symptom is coughing; and since it is highly contagious, it can sweep through an entire kennel in just a short period of time. A vaccination is a dog's best protection against this respiratory disease.

Leptospirosis is caused by bacteria that live in stagnant or slow-moving water. It is carried by rats and mice, and infection is begun by the dog licking substances contaminated by the urine or feces of infected animals. The symptoms are diarrhea and a yellowish-brownish discoloration of the jaws, tongue, and teeth, caused by an inflammation of the kidneys. This disease can be cured if caught in time, but it is best to ward it off with a vaccine which your veterinarian can administer.

Rabies is an acute disease of the dog's central nervous system. It is spread by infectious saliva transmitted by the bite of an infected animal. Rabies is generally manifested in one or the other of two groups of symptoms, and the symptoms usually appear within five days. The first is "furious rabies," in which the dog exhibits changes in his personality. The dog becomes hypersensitive and runs at and bites everything in sight. Eventually, the animal's lower jaw becomes paralyzed and hangs down; he walks with a stagger and saliva drips from his mouth. The second syndrome is referred to as "dumb rabies" and is characterized by the dog's walking in a bearlike manner, head down. The lower jaw is paralyzed, and the dog is unable to bite. Outwardly, it may seem as though he has a bone caught in his throat.

Even if your pet should be bitten by a rabid dog or other animal, he probably can be saved if you get him to the veterinarian in time for a series of injections. However, after the symptoms have appeared, no cure is possible. Remember that an annual rabies inoculation is almost certain protection against rabies. If you suspect that your dog or some other animal has rabies, notify your local health department. A rabid animal is a danger to all who come near him.

Canine parvovirus is a highly contagious viral disease that attacks the intestinal tract, white blood cells, and less frequently the heart muscle. It is believed to spread through dog-to-dog contact (the

Health and Disease

specific source of infection being the fecal matter of infected dogs), but it can also be transmitted from place to place on the hair and feet of infected dogs and by contact with contaminated cages, shoes, and the like. It is particularly hard to overcome because it is capable of existing in the environment for many months under varying conditions, unless strong disinfectants are used.

The symptoms are vomiting, fever, diarrhea (often blood-streaked), depression, loss of appetite, and dehydration. Death may occur in only two days. Puppies are hardest hit, with the virus being fatal to 75 percent of the puppies that contact it. Older dogs fare better; the disease is fatal to only two to three percent of those afflicted.

The best preventive measure for parvovirus is vaccination administered by your veterinarian. Precautionary measures individual pet owners can take include disinfecting the kennel and other areas where the dog is housed. One part sodium hypochlorite solution (household bleach) to 30 parts of water will do the job efficiently. Keep the dog from coming into contact with the fecal matter of other dogs when walking or exercising your pet.

Internal Parasites

There are four common internal parasites that may infect your dog. These are roundworms, hookworms, whipworms, and tapeworms. The first three can be diagnosed by laboratory examination; the presence of tapeworms is determined by seeing segments in the stool or attached to the hair around the tail. Do not under any circumstances attempt to worm your dog without the advice of your veterinarian. After first determining what type of worm or worms are present, he will advise you of the best method of treatment.

A dog or puppy in good physical condition is less susceptible to worm infestation than a weak dog. Proper sanitation and a nutritious diet help in preventing worms. One of the best preventive measures is to always have clean, dry bedding for

Adult whipworms are between two and three inches long, and the body of each worm is no thicker than a heavy sewing needle.

Health and Disease

your dog. This will diminish the possibility of reinfection due to flea or tick bites.

Heartworm infestation in dogs is passed by mosquitoes and can be a life-threatening problem. Dogs with the disease tire easily, have difficulty breathing, cough, and may lose weight despite a hearty appetite. If caught in the early stages, the disease can be effectively treated; however, the administration of daily preventive medicine throughout the spring, summer, and fall months is strongly advised. Your veterinarian must first take a blood sample from your dog to test for the presence of the disease. If the dog is heartworm-free, pills or liquid medicine can be prescribed that will protect against any infestation.

Above: Red mange mite.

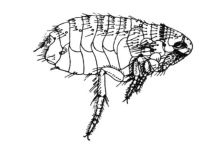

Below: The common dog flea.

A female dog tick that is gorged with blood.

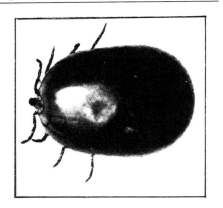

Below: The under side of a sarcoptic mange mite.

Health and Disease

External Parasites

Fleas and ticks are the two most common external parasites that can trouble a dog. Along with the general discomfort and irritation that they bring to a dog, these parasites can infest him with worms and disease. The flea is a carrier of tapeworm and may act as an intermediate host for heartworm. The tick can cause dermatitis and anemia, and it may also be a carrier of Rocky Mountain spotted fever and canine babesiasis, a blood infection. If your dog becomes infested with fleas, he should be treated with a medicated dip bath or some other medication recommended by your vet. Ticks should be removed with great care;

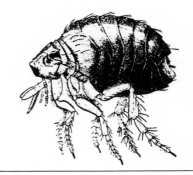

A sticktight flea.

you must be certain that the head of the tick is not left in the dog—this could be a source of infection.

Two types of mange, sarcoptic and follicular, are also caused by parasites. The former is by far the more common and results in an intense irritation, causing violent scratching. Close examination will reveal small red spots which become filled with pus. This is a highly

A female tick.

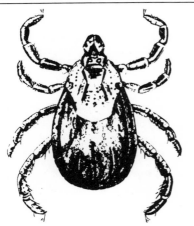

A male tick.

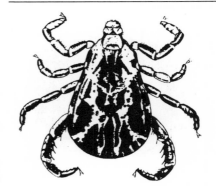

Health and Disease

contagious condition, and any dog showing signs of the disease should be isolated. Consult your veterinarian for the proper treatment procedures. Follicular mange is very much harder to cure; but fortunately, it is much rarer and less contagious. This disease will manifest itself as bare patches appearing in the skin, which becomes thickened and leathery. A complete cure from this condition is only rarely effected.

Other Health Problems

Hip dysplasia is an often crippling condition more prevalent in large

A dislocation of the upper leg bone. Dislocations should be immediately attended to by your vet.

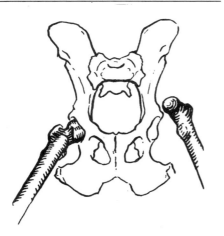

breeds than in small, but it has occurred in almost every breed. The cause is not known absolutely, though it is believed to be hereditary, and as yet there is no known cure. The condition exists in varying degrees of severity. In general, hip dysplasia can be described as a poor fit between the two bones of the hip joint and is caused by a malformation of one or the other. The condition causes stiffness in the hindlegs, considerable pain in the more severe cases, and difficulty of movement. It generally manifests itself in puppyhood and can be noticed by the time the young dog is two months old. If hip dysplasia is suspected, the dog should be x-rayed; and if afflicted, it should not be used for breeding. When the pain is severe and continual, euthanasia is occasionally recommended, though medication is available to control the pain and allow the dog to move with more ease.

Coughs, colds, bronchitis, and pneumonia are respiratory diseases that may affect the dog. Being subjected to cold or a draft after a bath, sleeping near an air conditioner or in the path of a fan, or resting near a radiator can cause respiratory ailments. The symptoms are similar to those in humans;

Health and Disease

however, the germs of these diseases are different and do not affect both dogs and humans, so they cannot be infected by each other. Treatment is much the same as for a child with the same type of illness. Keep the dog warm, quiet, and well fed. Your veterinarian has antibiotics and other remedies to help the dog recover.

Eczema is a disease that occurs most often in the summer months and affects the dog down the back, especially just above the root of the tail. It should not be confused with mange, as it is not caused by a parasite. One of the principle causes of eczema is improper nutrition, which makes the dog susceptible to disease. Hot, humid weather promotes the growth of bacteria, which can invade a susceptible dog and thereby cause skin irritation and lesions. It is imperative that the dog gets relief from the itching that is symptomatic of the disease, as self-mutilation by scratching will only help to spread the inflammation. Antibiotics may be necessary if a bacterial infection is, indeed, present.

Moist eczema, commonly referred to as "hot spots," is a rapidly appearing skin disease that produces a moist infection. Spots appear very suddenly and may spread rapidly in a few hours, infecting several parts of the body. These lesions are generally bacterially infected and are extremely itchy, which will cause the dog to scratch frantically and further damage the afflicted areas. Vomiting, fever, and an enlargement of the lymph nodes may occur. The infected areas must be clipped to the skin and thoroughly cleaned. Your veterinarian will prescribe an anti-inflammatory drug and antibiotics, as well as a soothing emollient to relieve itching.

The *eyes*, because of their sensitivity, are prone to injury and infection. Dogs that spend a great deal of time outdoors in heavily wooded areas may return from an exercise excursion with watery eyes, the result of brambles and high weeds scratching them. The eyes may also be irritated by dirt and other foreign matter. Should your dog's eyes appear red and watery, a mild solution can be mixed at home for a soothing washing. Your veterinarian will be able to tell you what percentage of boric acid, salt, or other medicinal compound to mix with water. You must monitor your dog's eyes after such a solution is administered; if the irritation persists, or if there is a significant discharge, immediate veterinary attention is warranted.

Your dog's *ears*, like his eyes, are extremely sensitive and can also be

Health and Disease

prone to infection, should wax and/or dirt be allowed to build up. Ear irritants may be present in the form of mites, soap or water, or foreign particles which the dog has come into contact with while romping through a wooded area. If your dog's ears are bothering him, you will know it—he will scratch his ears and shake his head, and the ears will have a foul-smelling dark secretion. This pasty secretion usually signals the onset of *otorrhea*, or ear canker, and at this stage proper veterinary care is essential if the dog's hearing is not to be permanently impaired. In the advanced stages of ear canker, tissue builds up within the ear, and the ear canal becomes blocked off, thus diminishing the hearing abilities of that ear. If this is to be prevented, you should wash your dog's ears, as they require it, with a very dilute solution of hydrogen peroxide and water, or an antibacterial ointment, as your vet suggests. In any case,

An ear mite.

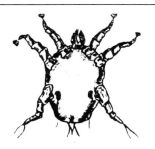

the ears, because of their delicacy, are to be washed gently, with a soft cloth or cotton.

Your pet's *teeth* can be maintained by his regular use of a chew product such as Nylabone® or Nylaball,® which serves to clean the teeth of tartar accumulation and to massage and stimulate the gums. Tartar accumulates on the teeth of dogs, particularly at the gum line, more rapidly than on the teeth of humans; and these accumulations, if not removed, bring irritation, infection and, ultimately, destruction of the teeth at the roots. With puppies, a chew product helps to relieve the discomfort of the teething stage and, of course, prevents the pup's chewing of your furniture and slippers! A periodic inspection of your dog's mouth will alert you to any problem he might have which would require a trip to the veterinarian's office. Any signs of tooth or gum sensitivity, redness, or swelling, signal the need for professional treatment.

A dog's *nails* should not be allowed to become overlong. If you live in a city and walk your dog regularly on pavement, chances are that his nails are kept trimmed from the "wear and tear" they receive from the sidewalks. However, if your dog gets all of his exercise in your yard, or if his nails simply

Health and Disease

grow rather quickly, it will occasionally be necessary for you to clip his nails. It is best for you to have your veterinarian show you the proper way to perform the nail clipping. Special care must always be taken to avoid cutting too far and reaching the "quick." If you cut into the quick of the nail, it will bleed, so it is easy to see why an expert must show you the proper procedure. A nail clipper designed especially for dogs can be purchased at any pet shop.

Emergency First Aid

If you fear that your dog has swallowed *poison*, immediately get him to the veterinarian's. Try to locate the source of poisoning; if he has swallowed, for example, a cleaning fluid kept in your house, check the bottle label to see if inducing the dog to vomit is necessary. Inducing the dog to vomit can be very harmful, depending upon the type of poison swallowed. Amateur diagnosis is very dangerous.

Accidents, unfortunately, do happen, so it is best to be prepared. If your dog gets hit by a car or has a bad fall, keep him absolutely quiet, move him as little as possible, and get veterinary treatment as soon as possible. It is unwise to give any stimulants such as brandy or other alcoholic liquids when there is visible external hemorrhage or the possibility of internal hemorrhaging.

Minor cuts and wounds will be licked by your dog, but you should treat such injuries as you would your own. Wash out the dirt and apply an antiseptic.

Severe cuts and wounds should be bandaged as tightly as possible to stop the bleeding. A wad of cotton may serve as a pressure bandage, which will ordinarily stop the flow of blood. Gauze wrapped around the cotton will hold it in place. Usually applying such pressure to a wound will sufficiently stop the blood flow; however, for severe bleeding, such as when an artery is cut, a tourniquet may be necessary. Apply a tourniquet between the injury and the heart if the bleeding is severe. To tighten the tourniquet, push a pencil through the bandage and twist it. Take your dog to a veterinarian immediately, since a tourniquet should not be left in place any longer than fifteen minutes.

Minor burns or scalds can be treated by clipping hair away from the affected area and then applying a paste of bicarbonate of soda and water. Apply it thickly to the burned area and try to keep the dog

Care of the Oldster

from licking it off.

Serious burns require the immediate attention of your veterinarian, as shock quickly follows such a burn. The dog should be kept quiet, wrapped in a blanket; and if he still shows signs of being chilled, use a hot-water bottle. Clean the burn gently, removing any foreign matter such as bits of lint, hair, grass, or dirt; and apply cold compresses. Act as quickly as possible. Prevent exposure to air by covering with gauze, cotton, and a loose bandage. To prevent the dog from interfering with the dressing, muzzle him and have someone stay with him until veterinary treatment is at hand.

Stings from wasps and bees are a hazard for the many dogs that enjoy trying to catch these insects. A sting frequently follows a successful catch, and it often occurs inside the mouth, which can be very serious. The best remedy is to get him to a veterinarian as soon as possible, but there are some precautionary measures to follow in the meantime. If the dog has been lucky enough to be stung only on the outside of the face, try to extricate the stinger; then swab the point of entry with a solution of bicarbonate of soda. In the case of a wasp sting, use vinegar or some other acidic food.

Barring accident or disease, your dog is apt to enjoy a life of 12 to 14 years. However, beginning roughly with the eighth year, there will be a gradual slowing down. And with this there are many problems of maintaining reasonably good health and comfort for all concerned.

While there is little or nothing that can be done in the instance of failing sight and hearing, proper management of the dog can minimize these losses. Fairly close and carefully supervised confinement are necessary in both cases. A blind dog, otherwise perfectly healthy and happy, can continue to be happy if he is always on a leash outdoors and guided so that he does not bump into things. Indoors, he will do well enough on his own. Dogs that are sightless seem to move around the house by their own radar system. They learn where objects are located; but once they do learn the pattern, care must be taken not to leave a piece of furniture out of its usual place.

Deafness again requires considerable confinement, especially in regard to motor traffic and similar hazards; but deafness curtails the dog's activities much less than blindness. It is not necessary to send any dog to the Great Beyond

Care of the Oldster

because it is blind or deaf—if it is otherwise healthy and seems to enjoy life.

Teeth in the aging dog should be watched carefully, not only for the pain they may cause the dog but also because they may poison the system without any local infection or pain. So watch carefully, especially when an old dog is eating. Any departure from his usual manner should make the teeth suspect at once. Have your veterinarian check the teeth frequently.

His System Slows Down

As the dog ages and slows down in his physical activity, so his whole system slows down. With the change, physical functions are in some instances slowed and in others accelerated—in effect, at least.

For example, constipation may occur; and bowel movements may become difficult, infrequent, or even painful. Chronic constipation is a problem for your veterinarian to deal with; but unless it is chronic, it is easily dealt with by adding a little extra melted fat to the regular food. Do not increase roughage or administer physics unless so directed by your veterinarian. If the added

fat in the food doesn't seem to be the answer to occasional constipation, give your dog a half or a full teaspoon of mineral oil two or three times a week. Otherwise, call your veterinarian.

On either side of the rectal opening just below the base of the tail are located the two anal glands. Occasionally these glands do not function properly and may cause the dog great discomfort if not cleaned out. This is a job for your veterinarian, until after he has shown you how to do it.

Watch His Weight

In feeding the aging dog, try to keep his weight down. He may want just as much to eat as ever, but with

An easy way to weigh your dog is to hold the dog while you stand on a scale, and then subtract your weight from the total.

Care of the Oldster

decreased activity he will tend to put on weight. This weight will tend to slow down all other bodily functions and place an added strain on the heart. So feed the same diet as usual, but watch the weight.

Age, with its relaxing of the muscles, frequently makes an otherwise clean dog begin to misbehave in the house, particularly so far as urination is concerned. There is little that can be done about it, if your veterinarian finds there is no infection present, except to give your dog more frequent chances to urinate and move his bowels. It's just a little bit more work on your part to keep your old friend more comfortable and a "good" dog.

Let your dog exercise as much as he wants to without encouraging him in any violent play. If he is especially sluggish, take him for a walk on a leash in the early morning or late evening. Avoid exercise for him during the heat of the day. And in cold weather or rain, try a sweater on him when he goes out. It's not "sissy" to put a coat on an old dog. You and your veterinarian, working closely together, can give your dog added life and comfort. So consult your veterinarian often.

Occasionally in an old dog there is a problem of unpleasant smell, both bodily and orally. If this situation is acute, it is all but unbearable to have the dog around. But the situation can be corrected or at least alleviated with frequent and rather heavy dosing of chlorophyll. A good rubdown with one of the dry-shampoo products is also helpful.

When the End Comes

People who have dogs are sooner or later faced with the tragedy of losing them. It's tough business losing a dog, no matter how many you may have at one time. And one dog never takes the place of another—so don't expect it to. When you lose your dog, get another as quickly as you can. It does help a lot.

Keep your dog alive as long as he is happy and comfortable. Do everything you reasonably can to keep him that way. But when the sad time comes that he is sick, always uncomfortable, or in some pain, it is your obligation then to have him put away. It is a tough ordeal to go through, but you owe it to your old friend to allow him to go to sleep. And, literally, that's just what he does. Your veterinarian knows what to do. And your good old dog, without pain, fright, bad taste, or bad smells, will just drift to sleep.

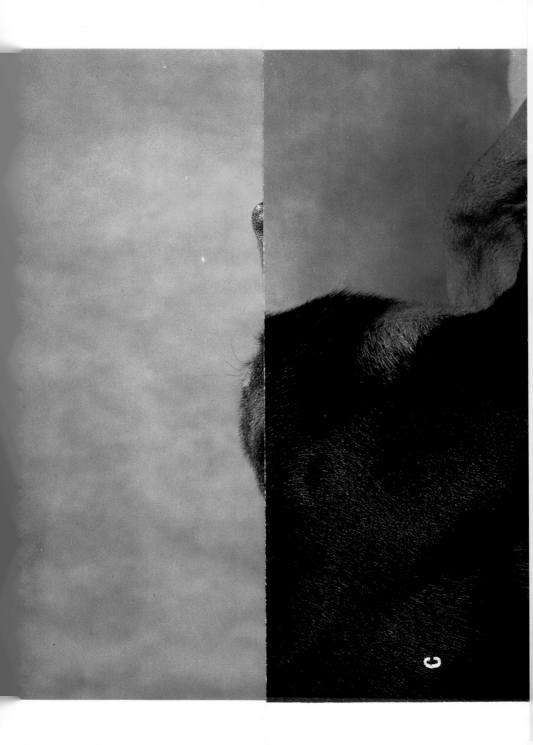